MODERN INDIAN THOUGHTS ON MATERIAL WORLD

MODERN INDIAN THOUGHTS ON MATERIAL WORLD

Arnabi Sen

KALPAZ

ISBN: 978-81-7835-962-5

Price : ₹ 450

First Published 2013

Published by

Kalpaz Publications
C-30, Satyawati Nagar,
Delhi - 110052
E-mail: kalpaz@hotmail.com Ph.: 9212142040

Laser Typesetting : Sanya Computers, Delhi
Printed at : G. Print Process, Delhi

Cataloging in Publication Data—DK
Courtesy: D.K. Agencies (P) Ltd. <docinfo@dkagencies.com>

Sen, Arnabi.
Modern Indian thoughts on material world / Arnabi Sen.
p. cm.
Includes bibliographical references (p.) and index.
ISBN 9788178359625

1. Materialism. 2. Philosophy, Indic. I. Title.

DDC 146.3 23

Dedicated to My Father

Contents

Preface

The aim of this book entitled *"The Modern Thoughts on Material World"* is to bring together the thoughts of ancient as well as modern Indian thinkers about the physical, material and consumer's world. Apart from the discussion of Indian Materialism and thoughts of Tagore, Gandhi and Aurobindo, we have tried to interpret the consumer's world. It has also been tried in this book to develop an idea of justified upbringing of the society in terms of proper use of our body and things around us. In this regard we have discussed the views of Tagore, Gandhi and Aurobindo on education in which they have expressed their realisation about the influence of material world on human beings and influence of human being on the natural as well as man-made material world. Both Gandhi and Tagore tried in their life to introduce handicraft as an essential part of life. If doing handicraft is essential the products of handicraft were also important for them.

Right from the very beginning of human reality man is related to the material world through his body which is itself a material object. Indian Philosophy on the whole considered human body and attachment to it as a source of *dukha*. Almost all the branches of Indian Philosophical schools except *Carvaka* consider human body as a bondage, as the soul due to *avidya,* grasps body, comes into contacts with material world and suffers.

By leaving aside the way to liberation or mukti, we tried to gauge the possibility of better human life, justified for both man and the material world on the one hand and for present and future on the other hand. Such atmosphere can be termed as *sarvamukti* in the terminology used by Sri Aurobindo.

In this book we have tried to point out that the seers, the prophets, the scientists, the industrialists, the artists are achieving higher and higher goals of life on the one hand but the common men on the other hand are suffering despite their honesty and dedication. It may not be *moksha* but a common man just wants to have humanitarian, empathetic world around him. This world seems to be the goal of the philosophical thoughts of

Tagore, Gandhi and Aurobindo. In the thoughts of these thinkers we find their deep concern about the misuse of things by us, the misconception of us about the material progress, the wrong aesthetic and ethical thinking of us and its repurcussions.

Acknowledgements

I acknowledge the help extended by many to enable me to accomplish the task. First I like to express my profound gratitude to UGC for funding the minor project under which I prepare the manuscript. I owe my profound gratitude to my former teacher and research guide Dr. Asha Mukherjee, Professor Visva Bharati, for encouraging me in this topic. I am indebted to Dr. Suman Jana Assoc. Professor in English, Vivekananda College Burdwan for informing me about the benefit of UGC Minor Project. I am indebted to my family members for helping me in various ways in completing the work.

Introduction

The aim of this Project is to bring together the Indian philosophical thoughts of Tagore, Gandhi, and Aurobindo on physical and material world and the thoughts of some modern writers on corporate world. Along with this an effort will be taken to gather some data of present day consumer world and its development by analysing them philosophically from the Indian philosophical view points. The Project incorporates another effort to develop a justified upbringing of the society through elementary education through Gandhi and Tagore's philosophy of education. Gandhi in his whole political as well as social life tried to bring about a change in education policy by developing a proper relation of man and things. Tagore on the other hand gave importance to the finer side of the human reality such as art and music and love for nature. So elementary education and vocational training remains as a point of discussion in this Project.

In order to bring out the man and thing relation, we "must first try to find out what meaning can be ascribed to the word 'thing'. According to Oxford dictionary, 'thing' can be inanimate object, belongings of some one, such as clothing accessories etc. at the same time things mean activity, action and thought. Things can be unspecified matters. Thing can be that which is needed, acceptable or fashionable. One's thing is his special interest. Thus in this book we consider things as the objects of the outside world thought, interest, fashion etc. Thing is that which is needed, so the food and tool we require and use are things, thus human body is a thing very much according to Indian spiritualism. In this way earth, water, air- all are things, in the same way money and power are also things.

Things by its dictionary meaning and philosophical interpretation are related to man or human reality right from the very beginning of the human reality. Even man's body is a thing. Indian Philosophy on the whole, excluding *Carvaka*, considers body as bondage of man. Indian Philosophy considers the whole world of things as the source of *dukha*. Man comes under the bondage, as the soul due to *avidya*, grasps a body and comes under the contacts of the material things and suffers. Thus

Mukti or *Moksha* is a possibility not for the man's "being in the world" (in Existentialistic terminology) but in the being beyond the world.

By leaving aside the way to liberation or *Mukti*, we have tried, here, to achieve a state where man can make his being in the world better, justified and humanitarian or noble. It may be termed as *Sarvamukti* which is liberation for all, not for an individual, so not merely *jivanmukti.* The Seers, the Prophets, the Scientist, the Industrialist, the Artists are attaining higher and higher goals on the one hand but the common man by leading a completely honest and dedicated life is suffering like anything in this world. If not *Moksha* but at least he can claim to have a humanitarian empathetic atmosphere around him. This atmosphere remains the goal of philosophy of Aurobindo Ghosh, Rabindranath Tagore and M.K. Gandhi. In their thoughts we can get an empathetic concern for the Nature which is considered as a thing in this book. In their thoughts we find their deep concern about the misuse of things, our misconception about material progress of the human society, our wrong aesthetic sense, our faulty idea about governance etc.

We will start our discussion by pointing out how Indian ancient philosophical schools deal with the physical world around us. Next we will discuss Aurobindo, Rabindranath and Gandhi who tried to give matter and material world its due respect; and importance. Our subject matter is divided in five chapters apart from Introduction and Conclusion. The first chapter entitled Indian Philosophy and Materialism contains Nyaya, *Vaisesika, Samkhya, Jaina, Bouddha* and *Vedanta* views of the physical world. The second chapter entitled The Spiritual Physical world has three sections in it for Aurobindo, Rabindranath and Gandhi. The third chapter entitled Common Men and The Material world is based on the contact programme, proposed to be carried out in this project, on the attitude of the different cultural groups of the society, towards the world of things. The fourth chapter entitled The Consumer World contains the analysis of the good and bad effects of the consumer world. The fifth chapter entitled The World as a Goal will try to develop an ideal humanistic account of man and thing relation on the basis of the contact programme and the thoughts of Aurobindo, Rabindranath and Gandhi.

1 Indian Philosophy and Materialism

Radhakrishnan says that Philosophy in India is essentially spiritual... "the Indian mind has traditionally exercised over the question of the Godhead, the end of life and the relation of the individual to the universal soul. Moreover in India, the interest of the philosophy, consists in the self of the man. If we put the subjective interest of the Indian mind alongwith its tendency to arrive at synthetic vision, we shall see how monistic idealism becomes the truth of the things."[1] Alongwith we can point out that the end or goal of life according to Indian Philosophy can't be achieved as long as matter sways spirit through its functions. Every code of Ethico-Spiritual discipline is so designed as to ensure gradual purification of the self from dominating effect of accumulated matter in the form of error, doubt, *vasana* and guarding the purified soul from the further inroads of the matter. Materialism of *Carvaka* system is just a foreign aberration rather than a full fledged of Indian Philosophy.

But from this it would be so simplistic a conclusion if it is said that there is no role of materialism in Indian Philosophy. Those who confused between religion and Philosophy are talking about liberation from the material world as *Moksha*. Indian Philosophy even Hindu philosophies revolt against ritualistic Hindu religion and *Moksha* might be a goal to Indian philosophy but it is not claimed to be attained surely and the Godhead is suppressed in philosophy as it is considered as a hindrance to enormous human possibility.[2] Hinduism, Buddhism and Jainism, these three religions are surely spiritualistic but some of their philosophical aspects are neither spiritual nor other worldly. Considering God as *Saguna Brahman*, as maya by *advaita* religion or rejecting the existence of uncaused cause or first cause by Buddhism and considering atoms as the house of eternal spirit by Jainism, they show that they are not professing spiritualism which is beyond human reality or beyond this physical world. *Samkhya* is silent about the existence of the God. *Vaisesika* and *Yoga* believe in the existence of a supreme being but do not consider Him to be the creator of the physical world, so the physical world is believed to have an independent existence.

Due to its belief in the monistic idealism as to represent the truth of all things, Indian Philosophy is considered not as a philosophy but as a religion. Identification of the Indian Philosophy with the single school of *Vedanta* makes it identified with the philosophy of *Maya* which indicates a negative attitude towards material world.[3] *Moksha* that is going beyond the physical and losing one's identity in a spiritual reality teaches inaction in the name of Philosophy.

Being influenced by the progress of the science the western philosopher Mr Flint said to regard matter merely as dirt is to forget that it is the wonderful work and glorious manifestation of God. Ignorance of the physical world and injustice to it, is even fatal to philosophy and theology.[4] Indian scholars too cannot remain unaffected by the growth of materialism as an ally of science. The expositor and the interpreter did not fail to respond altogether. In referring thoughts of Indian Philosophers between the years 1917-42, Dr P.T. Raju observes that divergent school of *Vedanta*. in their reappraisal of *Vedanta* they tried two things: (1) to be more accommodating to the material principles within its idealistic-spiritualistic framework, and (2) to recognise Indian Philosophy to be consisted of spiritualism and materialism as two independent "systems of thoughts".[5] R.N. Dutta believes that *Vedanta* teaches concrete spiritualism as opposed to Shankara's point of view which grants the world only an apparent reality. He declares Shankara's *Maya* theory as non-vedantic rather anti-vedantic.[6]

Realism which is allied to science is accepted by *Mimansa*, Jaina, *Sarvastivada* of Buddhism, *Carvaka*, Ramanuja, Madhava, Kashmira, Shaiva and even Shankara, when they talks about *vyavaharika satta*. For realism external world has to be accepted as extra-mental objective reality. Betty Heinman finds Indian Philosophy to accept empirical reality as contrasted with transcendental reality. *Maya* for him is conceptualised as *'sat'* as an empirical reality, *'asat'* as transcendental reality.[7] J.C. Chatterjee points out that Hindu realist always maintained that the ultimate constituents of the sensible things are indeed real, self-subsisting and independent of all percipients, but they are not solid hard particles with magnitude however small.[8] *Purva Mimansaka* emphatically denied that object is not solid extended or material. *Sankhya* accepts Material element as energy. Thus Hindu realism without materialistic consideration is confusing.

Dr P.R. Damle made a very good comment against identification of Indian Philosophy with spiritualism as he said it is to be a common fatal mistake of Indian spiritualism which has come in the way of our natural growth. Philosophy for Damle cannot prosper by ignoring materialism. He says that natural science and logic are not luxuries which Philosophy may or may not have but are in different ways constituents of philosophy and they can be ignored by Philosophy only at its own peril.[9]

M.N. Roy shows that defining Philosophy as a contemplative study of knowledge of Nature is satisfied by materialism only. Idealism or spiritualism place ultimate truth beyond the Ken of man who himself is a product of nature and limited by the law of nature. They make the world incomprehensible and lead us to no philosophy.[10]

Question is what is matter? Jacobi holds that matter is something that may become anything.[11] It means matter is atomic, Ubiquitous, solid, inert, impenetrable extension or wavy thought like energy, the reign of law.[12] Question is what specialty can Indian Materialism have? Max Muller said "What I admire in Indian Philosophy is that they never try to deceive us to their principles and consequences of their theories—they are bonafide Idealists or materialist, monist or dualist, theist or atheist because their reverence for truth is stronger than reverence for anything else."[13]

Materialism played a considerable role in Indian thoughts, more in the presupposition of science of Medicine (*Ayurveda*), Erotic (*Kamasutra*) and Politics (*Rajniti*) than in Philosophy. In many of literary composition, whether they form a part of epic or classical Sanskrit literature, the world affirming attitude (*pravritti*) is a natural outcome of materialistic outlook has been obviously upheld and eulogised as against the world negating attitude (*nivritti*). We can say that if materialism implies a world affirming attitude then apart from *Vedanta*, many other *astika* schools believe in the existence of the world as independent of the mind which tries to know it. The concept of padartha and dravya of *Nyaya-vaisesika* and affirmation of prakrti by *Samkhya* affirm material world. Dissociating oneself from *Prakrti* may be the way to liberation but no such claim is made in this philosophy that material world does not exist. *Nyaya-Vaisesika's padartha* has an epistemic value whereas *dravya* has a substantial existence as the material causes of the world. *Nyaya-Vaisesika's* claim for the existence of *Paramanu*, the eternal indivisible smallest particles, implies their belief in the indestructibility of the primary material cause of the material world. Now we can discuss different schools of Indian Philosophy and point out their world affirming attitude.

Carvaka—believes in a realistic and naturalistic empiricism and does not believe in the existence of anything that which is beyond the nature. World is not purposive for *Carvaka*. Nature or the world endures by itself. Along with the disbelief in the existence of the creator *Carvaka* denies the existence of *Adrsta, Karma, Niyati* etc. Things coming into being and going into non-being is thing's internal go. But things are not mysterious. Things are blindly constituted particles or matters.

But this lack of purpose in the creation and existence of the world does not contradict the purposive activity of men. The *Carvaka* therefore, gives importance to the realisation of the value of the human conduct for the fulfillment of the desire. Thus *Carvaka* develops a Materialistic Ethics of its own. *Carvaka* Ethics is materialistic not because it indulges in eating delicious food even by borrowing money. It is materialistic because it thinks it is matter not the soul is the source of our desire, life and longevity, as it says, *"javat jivet sukham jivet rnang krtva ghrtam pivet bhasmibhutasya dehasya punaragamanang kutah"* means while life remains let live happily being fed on ghee by running into debts, how the body that turns into ashes comes back. *Carvaka* realised the difficulty in achieving happiness. They believe in the strength and efficacy of man to attain happiness. One should avoid as well as endure pain to attain happiness. Growing of crops, building houses, cooking etc. might involve hazards but one has to undergo such activities to achieve happiness. *Carvaka* does not believe in body-torturing, ascetic or sacrificing activity prescribed in *Veda*. Among four ultimate goal of life such as *dharma, artha, kama, moksha, Carvaka* accepts artha and kama because *dharma* is vague and *moksha* is untrue.

Thus *Carvaka* is professing materialism by accepting perceptions and sensible as sole means and ground of knowledge. In ontology, by maintaining the ultimate reality to consist in four material substances earth, water, fire and air, in axiology, by denying teleology, *i.e.,* of a purpose behind the creation of the world, in Ethics, by upholding a hedonistic Ethics.

Buddhism—develops through some stages first, it is based on Buddha's teaching in *Tripitaka*, then in professing of *Sarvastivada* by *Vaibhasika* and *Soutantrika*, then on the basis of idealism of *Vijnanvada* or Nihilism of *Sunyavada*.

Another specialty of Buddhism consists in the vagueness of its metaphysics. He did not make it clear (I) whether the world is eternal or not; (II) whether it is finite or not; (III) whether soul and matter are one or not. This he did perhaps for the reason that he did not find above questions to be of practical use for his disciples. Buddha seems to hold the world not as eternal but as infinite. His concept of the chain of causality indicates the infiniteness of everything. But in so far as the eternality of the world is concerned Buddha did not believe in it. Buddha believes that by removing causes of existence it is possible to put an end in the cycle of the existence or *Bhavacakra*.

It is not the case for Buddha that the self is eternal. First of all self is not one with mind for Buddha. Self is a totality which speaks, thinks and feels and experiences the result of the activity of the whole world. Self is not only annihilated by death for Buddha, it is a fragmented entity divided in childhood, youth and oldage. Buddha's three main doctrines, *Aryasatyani, Pratityasamutpada* and *Astangikamarga* are neither spiritual nor material. Belief in *Aryasatyani, i.e.,* in the existence of *dukha* and possible ceasation does not relate it to any sort of immortality, God's grace or eternality. It is not also related to the world of things rather it is a dissociation from it which is suggested thereby. *Dukha* is believed to be caused by both material and spiritual belief by men. *Dukha* is caused by *jara-marana* and *jati* but the chain of cause starts by the *avidya* the *spiritual belief in immortality*. This ignorance for Buddha keeps man involved in birth cycle. *Astangikamarga* the eight fold path suggested by Buddha are mainly the habits of non-stealing, non-lying and non-killing which may be interpreted as spiritual but in actuality these are habits of mind and body which lead to the perfect physical and mental ease at the last stage of eight fold path. The theory *pratityasamutpada* is claimed by the scholar to oppose naturalism or *svabhavavada* since nothing can be said to possess independent quality, *svabhava* since everything is caused by the prior thing or a chain things. But on the other hand very much like *svabhavavada, pratityasamutpada* stands for the uniformity of the nature and ordered succession. Along with this rejection of the existence of any mysterious uncaused entity is a rejection of spiritualism. For Buddha the cosmos is Godless (*anissara*), impermanent (*adhuva*) and completely lacking of any transcendental substance (*una*) in it.

But unlike naturalism Buddha does not believe in any necessary relation between cause and effect. He did not believe in *satkaryavada* or *asatkaryvada*. It seems that Buddha did not concern himself about the beginning of the existence but about the possibility of the end of the existence by removing the cause. In order to avoid such destructive attitude in Philosophy Buddha's disciples propagated theories such as *ksanikattavada* and *sunyavada* and professed in favour of *sarvastvada* which is more realistic and naturalistic.[14] Stcherbatsky shows that in the theories of *Vaibhasika* and *Soutantrika, i.e.,* in vahyatapratyaksavada and in vahyanu-meyavada knowledge is upheld as complex phenomena in which several element including consciousness exists separately but interconnected.[15] The nature of consciousness is empirical in Buddhist psychology. For J.N. Sinha it is a relation between subject and object. Each psychosis is awakened by eternal stimulus the stimulus ceases the psychosis ceases. But for this reason Buddhism cannot be said to be Materialistic. A materialist is monist who concentrates on the physical nature of all atoms while Buddhists are radical pluralists. The pluralism is not of substance but of forces *i.e.,* of happening and events, upheld everything as change and becoming. Thus selves as well as things, objects, life and world consisted of eternal forces comes within the nexus of change and becoming. Thus which are really separate may be mistaken for identity a combination may give rise to the illusory existence of the selves and things.

We can conclude that Buddhism on the whole is not materialism but not spiritualism either. But by denying the existence of substance, self and eternality of God, a philosophy cannot be said to dualism of spiritualism and materialism. In so far as our motto of bringing out man thing relation, is concerned, we can say that in Buddhism relation is reveled as an illusory or ignorant; relation. Thing is altogether missing in Buddhism but there is no effort to dissociate self from things by considering self as pure and eternal but capable of being wise and liberated from the cycle of birth. Through perception and inference the two means of knowledge nothing can be known as things for Buddhism, only a force of happening can be experienced by the consciousness which itself is a part of the force. Thus neither consciousness nor object has substantial existence in Buddhism.

Jainism—Aims to resolve Metaphysical problem by materialistic solution. Like other spiritual philosophy matter is taken as identical with the cause of bondage and evil. Thus Jainism too stands in between spiritualism and materialism. It is representing a pluralistic realism accepting reality of both soul and matter. It believes in the reality of *karma, jiva and kriya, i.e.,* in the reality of the matter, soul and action and in relation between soul and matter. Cosmology in this philosophy is considered as a system which starts from nothing, so no creator of the world is believed to exist in this philosophy. World for them is a beginning less play and interaction between matter and soul. Even soul in its omniscient state and *Kevalajnana* finds material object as its data according to Umasvati and Jinabhadra, the famous Jaina commentators.

It is true that matters proper or pudgala is not the only reality for Jainism, it is a subdivision of *ajiva*, and other subdivisions are *dharma*, *adharma, aksa, kala* which are not materialistic in nature. *Jiva* on the other hand opposed to materials. But B.M. Barua holds that except *kala* all other categories according to Jainism are *astikayas*[16] which literary means a body that which is extended. So a materialistic flavour we get in Jainism's description of being. Even *kala* is a substance for Jaina which understood as a thing by common sense. *Pudgala*, or matter according to *Kundakundacarya* are enjoyable by senses, body and mind.[17] It is eternal, atomic, indeterminate, a mere something and liable to be anything.[18] Jaina materialism include karma even in matter. *Karma* is not mystical unseen force to them. Rather it is an energy which rouses passion and emotion in *jiva*, it is an activity of attraction towards object and responsible for weighing down *jiva*, Umaswati explains karma not only as material but atomic in character. H. Jacobi gave three reasons in favour of considering *karma* as material. His reasons are: (I) Soul is light, it goes above matter, but *karma* weighs it down; (II) soul assumes colour according to *karma;* (III) *Karma* can assume various forms.

Akasa, in jaina's interpretation gets sound in it because of violent contact between two objects. *Akasa* at the same time provides room to all other substances. *Kala* is atomic in character, innumerable in number and every one of it is connected with pradesa of *lokakasa*. Amrtacandra suri says *"dharma, adharma* and *akasa* are each single *dravya* whereas time matter and soul are held to be innumerable *dravyas*.[19]

Jaina conception of self is based on the experience of life. They did not believe in eternal immutable change in a world of changing phenomena. *Jiva* is nothing more than a living body and mind, speech activity and instrumentality thereby. Thus *jiva* becomes a quasi-material substance. Jaina doesn't believe in separation between soul and body. Jaina believes that there is infinite number of bound souls, bound in the body and a large number of souls are not participating in the activity of life. They are reserved which fills the gap of liberated soul liberated through action. Thus liberation is analogous to the material entity or special-occupants. The souls that occupy the body of plant are called *nitya-nigodha* are hardly distinguishable from material things. Jaina believes that souls do not reside only in organic matter but also in apparently dead matter. Existence of earth-body's soul, fire soul, soul in the drop of the water soul of the wind atoms are believed by Jainas.

Soul is same size of the body, it occupies it, it dies as body dies. Soul suffers the pleasures and injuries of the body. If soul is said to be the essence of the body, it is like fire in the wood, oil in the oil seed and like butter in the milk. For liberated souls Jaina holds that it becomes two third of the size of the body it had last. Belief in the retention in the soul even after liberation is obviously a sign of materialistic bent of Jaina despite they professed separation between soul and matter. Thus in Jaina Ethics also we find materialism to play a considerable role in it. The *triratna* of Jaina ethical thought, *i.e.*, to pursue *samyak darsana, samyak jnana* and *samyak caritra* are all aimed at mortification of flesh, *i.e.*, to reject care, comfort, shelter, food and clothes for the body.

So apart from its ethics Jaina philosophy is materialistic in so far as Jaina epistemology, ontology, axiology and cosmology are concerned. Only in suggesting ethical discipline they are suggesting some ascetism.

Nayaya-vaisesika—The thought was-born for the hostility against Buddhist doctrine of flux and professed doctrine of substance with their qualities and particularities for Radhakrishnan. This attitude expressed materialistic attitude instead of Buddhist idealism.

Nyaya the joint school of *vaisesika* recommends the study of sixteen topics neither of them suggest highly spiritual end to be achieved. The topic's names themselves show their non-spiritual nature. The names are *pramana, prameya, samasya, projna, drstanta, siddhanta, avayava, tarka, nirnaya, vada, jalpa,* etc. thus *Nayaya* is study for knowledge with reasoning without upholding ways to the liberation. Kalidas Bhattacharya rightly pointed out that *Nayaya-Vaisesika* theory of knowledge is free from mysticism. Nothing is recognised as purely subjective, as self luminating.[20] They did not distinguish between *atma* and *paramatma.* They include god in their ontology all of a sudden being influenced by *Yoga* school, discussed in detail but God or theology did not become an integral part of their philosophy. Apart form discussing or accepting the concept of *Moksha Nyaya-Vaisesika* preferred to discuss the contrast between the unconscious, painlessness and conscious experience of joy in our common ordinary life.

In *Nyaya-Vaisesika* epistemology we can see that perception is the basic *pramana* and all other *pramanas* such as inference and testimony are based on the perception itself. Inference is based on the perceptual knowledge of *vyapti* the invariable concomitance two things and *sabda* is based on trustworthy person who becomes trustworthy on inference and inference is based on perception. Moreover, the knowing subject or self is not the fountain head of consciousness for *nyaya-vaisesika* and therefore the supreme self or God is not the fountain head of all knowledge. Kalidas Bhattacharya pointed out that the self in *nyaya-vaisesika* never means a knower but only a locus where mental states are said to occur. Self does not know anything, unless mind or sense organs come into contact with object. Moreover the soul and mind according to *vaisesika* come under the category of substance.

In this philosophy existence is foremost characteristic of the substance known through qualities and actions which are directly apprehended. Thus all other categories apart from substance with its qualities and action namely generality particularity and inherence and even *abhava* are relatively real as related to substance. God is neither mentioned nor discussed or we can see a cryptic mention of it. About *Moksha Nyaya-Vaisesika* philosophy is non-materialistic as the blissfulness which is the goal of *Moksha* is not to achieve material happiness.

In conclusion we can say that though the feature of reality upheld by *Nyaya-vaisesika* school is showing a total acceptance of entire cosmos and its matter and action but in so far as *Mukti* or *Moksha* is concerned it can be achieved without achieving a material end. *Moksha* is not *abhyudaya* but *nihsreyasa* which is logically irrelevant to their epistemology, ontology, logic and cosmology.

Samkhya-yoga—The first rationalistic philosophy of the world laid down the scientific thought in India it is not ofcource a thorough going materialism but a combination of Idealism and Dualism. It seems that Samkhya upheld idealism for *purusa* the soul and materialism for *prakrti*. Pure soul is free from materials as well as it is free from ignorance and dissociated from *prakrti*. On the other hand *prakrti* is an independent material existence free from any attachment with the soul. *Purusa* gets bound in *prakrti* due to its ignorance and nearness to *prakrti* whereas *purusa's mukti* can be achieved by dissociation from *prakrti*. But a full-fledged discussion of *prakrti's* evolution shows that matter and its changes are not regarded as unreal or illusion like *vedantin's*.

There is no stage in Samkhya philosophy where matter is treated as non-existent. Samkhya never treated that matter and bondage of *purusa* are partial appearance of the prakrti which disappears with the onset of cognition. Vijnanabhiksu comments that cut and dried monism of *Upanisad* is meant for ordinary men who are not gifted to have discriminative knowledge.[21] He also commented that Vedantic monism is nothing but non-separation of *prakrti* and *purusa* in space. Radhakrishnan holds that there is no stage in Samkhya philosophy identified with spiritualism.[22] At the same time Jacobi holds that insistence on the absolute reality and independence of spirit the Samkhya went against materialism. Even D.P. Chattopadhyaya admits that we cannot ignore Samkhyans insistence on the reality of *purusa*.[23]

Another point must be raised that in this philosophy no effort has been made to prove uncaused, unmanifested cause of the *prakrti* to be more real than the world manifested. Rather the school based its argument in favour of the existence of *prakrti* on the reality of the world. There is no distinction between *gunas* and origin of *gunas*. The evolution may be thought to be caused by the nearness of *purusa* to *prakrti* but it is not claimed by the school that *Prakrti* needs outside agency to have motion in it motion is inherent in *prakrti*.

From epistemological point of view the dualism between *prakrti* and *purusa* is not conclusion of a metaphysical doctrine but of an Ethics and Morality that recognises man's suffering and the way to get rid of them. Moreover, *purusa* in Samkhian concept is non-doer, non-enjoyer. Question arises how can *purusa* be the cause of evolution? *Purusa* is described in Samkhya philosophy as innumerable but the determining factors of multiplicity of *purusa* such birth, death and sense endowment are all material and non-spiritual. Perception as the basic means of knowledge proves the involved character and plurality of *purusa*. *Purusa* represents the soul of an ordinary individual acting and being acted upon, undergoing changes of itself and its counter part *prakrti*. Thus apart from the Independent and fundamental status of *prakrti pradhanakaranatavada* and *svabhavavada* believed to be the characteristic if *prakrti* rendering Samkhya to be materialistic in this regard, if the school is professing dualism of *prakrti* and *purusa* then there is no place of God in it so samkhya could not uphold any clear concept of god in their philosophy.

The role assigned to *Samkhya Yoga* dualism of *purusa* and *prakrti* is of self revealing. Thus *purusa-sannidhi* or nearness of *purusa* to *prakrti* is not based on solid reason. Birth-cycle or ignorance of believing in immortality is considered In Buddhism as the cause of *dukha*. In *Vedanta. Maya* or belief in the truth of the matter is considered as reason of bondage. No such reason is there in *Samkhya-Vaisesika* philosophy for *purusa sannidhi*. Moreover it is said to occur when *purusa* is free not bound. In Buddhism and *Vedanta* ignorant and bound soul comes in contact with world or matter. In Samkhian thought bondage comes to the free soul when it has contact with *prakrti*.

Vedanta—World is not denied but has no spiritual significance but has a practical significance indeed. The construction of the *prakrti* is described as *Maya* in *Vedanta*. An inferior role is assigned to *prakrti* as an illusion. *Maya* or the construction of the world has no independent existence apart from *Brahman*. This *Brahman* is not the all powerful lord. For Shankara, lord itself is the product of *Maya* so cannot be the cause of *Maya* or the world. Shankara does not consider world as a permanent *Maya*, can be removed through right knowledge which does not mean that world may disappear. Rather with the advent of right knowledge and removal of *Maya* an identity between the world and *Brahman* will be revealed to the consciousness. So the world identical to *Brahman* is real and world different from *Brahman* is unreal. So there can be two different views on the reality, one is worldly view and another is a view conscious of *Brahman*. But both of the views are the views of the man who considers himself either in the world or as the world. Shankara does not find any possibility of putting an end to the infinity of the world like Buddha. He seems to believe that the world will remain eternally if world is realised to be the expression of eternal, universal, impersonal principle.

Question arises that if according to *Vedanta*, spiritual principle is the sole reality then how to account for material multiple object of the world. For Shankara material multiple objects has no future, whereas for Ramanuja these are the expression of highest spiritual principle as cit and acit and mind and matter.

For Shankara, world is neither one nor many, all its births and deaths, production, destruction, every incidents of bondage and liberation has no real significance. There is no actual change in this world. No relation like causality exists in this world; World is for Shankara beginning less yet has an end *Moksha* which has a beginning yet no end can be proved.

It must be pointed out that *avidya* and ignorance as synonymous with *Maya* is not indicating any subjective or mental failure to know the reality but *Maya* is objective state of material cause of the manifested world.

Ramanuja agrees with Shankara that nothing is outside *Brahman*, but he believes that neither matter nor mind is unreal, rather these all are included in *Brahman*. If *Brahman* is all exclusive in Shankara's *Vedanta* it is all inclusive in Ramanuja's *Vedanta*. Ramanuja's *Brahman* is a God united with the matter but not identical with the soul and matter. *Traividdhasattva, i.e., sattva, raja, tama* constitute soul and matter but god is constituted only by *suddhasatta* revealed as *sattva*. Thus matter in Ramanuja's thought is insubstantial in character and a mere attribute of substance. Thus Ramanuja's philosophy has nothing material in it.

Nimbarka clearly says that *Brahman* transforms itself into the world of plurality just as milk transforms itself into curd. *Brahman* turns out to be a real efficient as well as material cause of the world.

Thus a spirit behind or in all sorts of appearance is thought to exist for all the *Vedantins*. No materialism is there in *Vedanta* as the material world itself is considered as identical to but unknown as *Brahman*. It seems that the materiality we ascribe to object is not the material in actual sense in is quite real and eternal as spirituality is. In the next chapters we will try to develop a similar views that materiality is not to be taken for granted, it should be granted by Its proper place in human life it totally intermingled with all the aspects of human life.

In our discussion on Materialism what we have seen so far is that Indian philosophical schools did not want to make their philosophy materialistic except *Carvaka*. But some times their handling of the thought leaves some possibility to interpret their Philosophies as inclined to materialism. But earth, water, fire, air, *jada, pudgala, prakrti,* causality, evolution which are treated as basic elements or features of the reality, belong to the physical world not spiritual world. Thus Indian philosophy may not be materialistic but very much close to the nature, not merely an intellectual exercise.

References

1. Indian Philosophy, Radhakrishnan, pp. 14-31.
2. Outlines of Indian Philosophy, M. Hiriyana, pp. 17-19.

3. Vedantic Attitude Towards Matter, Hindustan Review IXXIV (1941-1942), p. 30.
4. Anti Theistic Theory Robert Flint (Baird Lecture 1877), p. 40.
5. Progress of Indian Studies survey : (1917-42), Indian Philosophy, P.T. Raju, Ed. R.N. Dhndekar, p. 398.
6. Last Chapter, The *Vedannta*, N. Dutta.
7. ff, Reality of fiction in hindu thought, Betty Heinman, Dr Bhandarkar Volume, and Ed. B.C. Law, p. 97.
8. Hindu Realism, J.C. Chatterjee, p. 24.
9. Philosophical Essays, P.R. Damle, pp. 196-98.
10. Materialism and Human Knowing, Roy, Wood, Sellers, pp. 81-91.
11. Naturalism and the Nature of Things, PR LIII 1944, p. 437.
12. Ch. I, Modern Science and Materialism, Bertrand Russell, p. 20.
13. SSIP Introduction, p. 11.
14. Materialism in Indian thought, K.K. Mittal, p. 149.
15. The Central Conception of Buddhism and The Meaning of the Word Dharma, p. 4.
16. Materialism in Indian Thought, K.K. Mittal, p. 119.
17. *Ibid.*, p. 120.
18. The Metaphysics and Ethics of Jaina, Jacobi, p. 168.
19. Materialism in Indian Thought, K.K. Mittal, p. 124.
20. Materialism in Indian Thought, K.K. Mittal, p. 169.
21. Materialism in Indian thought, K.K. Mittal, p. 208.
22. *Ibid.*, p. 211.
23. Lokayata Darsana, pp. 362-63.

2 The Spiritual-Physical World

The closeness of Indian philosophy to *prakrti* inspired thinkers like Tagore and Gandhi and their philosophy a lot. They consider matter and material world not something to be looked down upon but too much dependence on the material world and ignoring spiritual and ethical aspects of life also considered by them as to live a life of beast. In Aurobindo's philosophy we find that spirituality comes into existence through physical and material world but liable to rise above. All three philosophers do not consider the human race fit for industrial and commercial development. Either they find it to be an artificial development or a mere accumulation of money and power. Since such development is not development of that which is inside us. Industrial development results into accumulation of huge amount of money by a small section of the society. Now we will discuss the thought and principle upheld by Aurobindo, Rabindrnath and Gandhi separately.

Section: (I) Aurobindo Ghosh does not believe in dualism between spiritualism and materialism for him if reality is spiritual then matter is also spiritual, for him there is no way to spirit to appear in this world without the medium of matter. He says, "The affirmation of a divine life upon earth and an immortal sense in mortal existence can have no base unless we recognise not only eternal spirit as an inhabitant of this bodily mansion, but accept matter of which it is made, as a fit or noble material out of which He weaves constantly His garbs, builds recurrently the unending series of His mansion.[1]

Thus Aurobindo disproves both materialistic denial of spiritualism and spiritualistic negation of matter. If matter is claimed to be scientifically discovered as the only reality then Aurobindo will ask not to overlook scientific spirit which knows no halting place, knows the limitation of intellect. Thus there is no finality of scientific conclusion and therefore of the materialistic denial. Aurobindo says, "...the claim of pure spirit manifest in us its absolute freedom and the claim of universal matter to be the mould and condition of our manifestation, we have to find a truth that can give to both, their due portion in life, their due justification in thought."[2]

Reality for Aurobindo is *sacchidananda*, means in his interpretation, the pure existence (*sat*), the conscious force (*cit*) and the delight of existence or bliss (*anada*). One may understand by this meaning that there is a place of matter in reality conceived by Aurobindo. But he says clearly that "Matter is the form of substance of being which the existence of sacchidananda assumes when it subjects itself to this phenomenal action of its own consciousness and force."[3] It seems that for Aurobindo reality appears as a matter but he did not profess any *avedattva* (identity) between matter and spirit. Pure existence is divine whereas material world is cosmic world, there is a gap between iwo. But despite the difference between spirit and matter, Aurobindo says, "...divine descends from the pure existence through the play of conscious force and bliss and the creative medium of super mind into Cosmic Being, we ascend from matter through developing life, soul and mind and the illumination medium of super mind towards the divine being"[4]

Question arises, what Aurobindo means by descent and ascent. Descent means involution and ascent means evolution. One is the reverse method of other. Involution means creation. He finds this creation necessary for an order and shape to be brought about in this world. So he says, "Infinite consciousness in its finite action can produce oniy infinite results; to settle upon a fixed truth or order of truths and build a world in conformity with that which is fixed, demands a selective faculty of knowledge commissioned to shape finite appearance out of infinite reality."[5] Creation for Aurobindo belongs to the reality, a stage of reality, a stage of divine descend in this world. The meaning Aurobindo ascribes to the evolution makes it clear that it is stage of creation. Evolution for Aurobindo is the last stage of involution or creation. He says, "Spirit is a final evolutionary emergence because it is the original involutionary element and factor. Evolution is the inverse action of the involution: what is ultimate and last derivation in the involution is the first to appear in the evolution. What was original and the primal in the involution, is in the evolution the last supreme emergence."[6]

Now we can make it clear what does Aurobindo mean by the 'selective faculty of knowledge' which is shaping finite appearance from infinite realty. Aurobindo holds that creation is a plunge of spirit into ignorance. It is the power of Divine for him, to withhold itself partially. Thus selective faculty is synonymous with ignorance. Ignorance for Aurobindo is a part of knowledge but may be the unknown part of knowledge because Aurobindo says, "Ignorance is seeking and preparing to transform itseif by a progressive illumination of its darkness into the knowledge that is already conceived in it."[7] But Aurobindo sees this unknowing part; not as being forced into consciousness but comes as a, stage in progressive illumination. He also says, "Ignorance must be—a development of consciousness, knowingly adapted, to which it is not forcibly subjected but which is used for its cosmic purpose."[8] Then question arises, why Aurobindo describes it as ignorance. Aurobindo holds that such selective faculty of knowledge is partial, purposive and egoistic. He says, "builds a wall of separation which shuts out the consciousness in each form, from the awareness of its total self"[9] he also says, "...we take our limited egoistic mentality, vitality, corporeality for our true self and regard everything other than that, as not self."[10]

Now the question is what kind of self is true self? It seems to be an individual self opposite of collective self. The self which is for one's own enjoyment and involved in utilising its capacity as much as possible. It is not the group self where individual interest is sacrificed or submerged. Aurobindo describes it as true self as he finds it to be confined into one's own self and not to go out of one's self. But it should not be understood that Aurobindo prefers this self instead of the group self rather he prefers the opposite one, but consider true self a necessary stage of human development Aurobindo thinks that such true self is the production of modern science. He says, "...the first object of life—is for the individual to survive as long as he may, to become strong efficient powerful, to dominate his environment and his fellows to raise himself on his strenuous and egoistic line to his full stature of capacity and reap his full measure of enjoyment."[11] Such view of life is influenced by the growth of modern science for Aurobindo. He says, "Science discovered the root nature of all living is a struggle to take best advantage of the environment for self preservation, self-fulfillment, self-aggrandisement."[12]

Thus modern science created, for Aurobindo, an 'exaggerated individualism' on the one hand and on the other hand, as Aurobindo says, "...what nature seeks to preserve is not the individual but the type and in her scale of values takes precedence of human group over the individual human being"[13] Aurobindo finds two views of life subjective and objective, subjective views proceeds from within by developing a self-consciousness and result into self shaping. Whereas objective views proceeds by a look at the world as a thing—in this view the world is viewed as a law out side oneself."[14]

But Aurobindo raised question about the truth of the self and for its real abiding place. We may find the truth in individual self consciousness or in collective self Aurobindo thinks about another self which is an enlarged one. He says, "We may enlarge the idea of the self and as objective sees the universal force of nature which is the one reality and of which every thing is the process, we may come subjectively to the realisation of a universal Being or Existence which fulfils itself in the world and the individual and the group with an impartial regard for all as equal powers of its self manifestation—the subjective search for the self may, like objective, lean preponderantly to identification with the conscious physical life because the body is or seems to be the frame and determinant here of the mental and vital movement and capacities."[15] Therefore, physical force is the abiding place of the self, emerging out of which self can realise the universal 'Being' or 'Existence'. Aurobindo finds the similar process in the nature which comes into existence through the physical world. He says, "Nature starts from matter—releases out of involution in life all the crude material of mind and when he is ready, turns mind upon itself and upon life and matter in a great mental to understand all three in their phenomena...."[16]

Aurobindo finds culture to be the pursuit of mental life, mental life is made up of three elements for Aurobindo, which are sense and emotion, active dynamic elements, ethical, aesthetic life and intelligence. Aurobindo thinks this mental life to be a chaotic war of ideas, impulses, tendencies which perplex efforts. But in complexity even man forms a large idea of culture. Aurobindo distinguished culture from civilisation, it seems from Aurobindo's discussion that civilisation can be prior to culture. Proper civilisation can bring about proper culture by making a proper mental life. Aurobindo says "...in a civilised society there is still the distinction between the partially, crudely, conventionally civilised and the cultured. It would seem therefore that mere participation in the ordinary benefits of civilisation is no enough to raise man into the mental life proper...."[17]

Aurobindo thinks that in improper mental life or improper culture, man is more ethical than aesthetic, but his ethical life is not governed by reason but appeared by intelligence which is not his own but of a group mind. The use of this intelligence brings no development in him than his daily movement. He can be a developed physical or economic man but not mentally active. But the man which is awakened by necessity of Being, educated by new information and new ideas is trying to be mentally active. He knows that he has to think about ethical, social, religious and scientific problems. He may read poems he may not have aesthetic ideas, but appreciates art. He reads news paper, public reviews, appreciates cinemas, theatres. Such man for Aurobindo achieves something as he says, "Science hastens to bring her knowledge and discoveries to his doors and equip his life with endless machinery; politics are shaped in his image... If a Lenin, a Mussolini, a Hitler have achieved their rapid and stupefying success, it was because this driving force, this quick responsive acting mass was there to carry them to victory—a force lacking to their less fortunate predecessors."[18]

Aurobindo thinks even this mentally active man cannot achieve a best mind directed by reason or intelligent will. Aurobindo finds commercialism to be the heart of this civilisation which has made necessary to man the things to which he was not accustomed in terms of occupation, emotion, ideology, and aestheticism. Such man has a thirst for general information of all kinds not because he cares to co-ordinate or assimilates, but because they are the part of the popular notion, provided they are presented before him with a brilliant and exciting manner and add colour to his life. Though such activism belongs to some crude mental being but much more open and free it has democratised culture. Aurobindo says, "The higher mental life in a world has been democratised, activised with good and bad result. Through it all the eye of faith can see perhaps that a yet crude but enormous change has begun. Thought and knowledge, if not yet beauty, can get a hearing and even produce rapidly some large, vague yet in the end effective will for their result"[19]

Aurobindo finds that such information in education and social system will create an "unknown phenomenon of race of men—not only a class—who have to some extent found and developed their mental selves a cultured humanity." But Aurobindo thinks that only a ordered practice of culture with a gross, vital, commercial view, with a civilisation of 'abundant and even redundant' apparatus even with gross vital success cannot promise or realise a cultured humanity. Aurobindo holds that the 'unmental' physical, 'unintellectualised' vital, the crude economic and grossly domestic life is barbarism just opposite of cultured life. But Aurobindo also says, "Even a developed nation developed within itself, knowledge and science and arts, but still in its general outlook, its habits of life of thought content to be governed not by knowledge and truth and beauty and high ideals of living but by gross vital, commercial, economic view of existence—that nation or age may be civilised in a sense, but it is not the realisation or promise of cultured humanity—a society following such a rule of life may be..... vigorous, descent, well ordered, successful, religious, moral but it is prison which human soul has to break."[20] Aurobindo did not find, the Athenian life dominated for centuries with art, drama, poetry, philosophy, music, architecture and sculpture, to be dominated by moral order. But moral order, for the maintenance of so social life is not enough without social discipline. Thus Aurobindo says, "Neither can ethical being nor aesthetic being is the whole man,—they are merely—two power full elements—these two powers of psychological being which present in us the essential principle of energy and essential principle of delight— tapas and ananda—can be thus helped by each other, the one to a richer the other to a greater self expression."[21]

We have seen in the philosophy of Aurobindo so far that both ethical and aesthetic lives of men with gross vital, domestic, commercial tendencies are representing the phenomenon of a 'race of men.' It is not a class. Individuality either lost in it or achieves thai which is handed over to them by the mass of the people as Mussolini, Lenin, Hitler etc. achieved. But Aurobindo finds strife between individual and group tendencies. Aurobindo holds that historically or sociologically we can see individual to be subservient under the group. In human evolution Aurobindo says, "He begins with uniformity and subservience of the individual and proceeds towards variety and freedom of Individual."[22] He also says, that in matter uniformity is the sign of the group; free variation and individual development progress with the growth of life and mind. If then we suppose man to be a mental being in matters and out of matter we assume that he begins with uniformity and' subservience of the individual and proceeds towards variety and freedom of the individual"[23]

Thus we can have a humanistic and socialistic interpretation of Aurobindo's concept of descend and ascend. By coming down of individual in group life or ordered life and emerging with freedom and variety. Modern states dominate individual ego for a collective interest, mainly by organising vital and economic arrangement. Aurobindo says, "In modern times the state—demands, individual egoism shall immolates itself to a collective interest—its way to perfection lies through the ordering by the state of all the economic and vital arrangements of the individual and the group."[24] Thus we can say that the state run by the involution or descend. It is a materialisation of the individual by reducing ic into a group. All the activities of state is to reduce individuality no matter it is financial or executive or judicial. Aurobindo says, "The financial power carries with it the control of public purse and the expenditure of the wealth contributed by the society or the national purposes—must pass into the hands of—authority, has taken up the business of organising and making efficient the united action of community."[25]

Aurobindo considered economic unity for an important task of the nation. Aurobindo finds such economic authority or state to the requirement of modern society. He says, "...in the growing unity of mankind the evolution of such authority must become an early and pursuing need. The world state.....must begin not only to concentrate military force in hands, but commence curiously in the beginning—the ordering of the commercial, industrial and economic life of the race and control at first, no doubt, only of the principal relation of international commerce. Since industry and trade are now five-sixth of the society, a world state which did not control human life in its chief principle and its largest activity will exist only in name."[26] Apart from economic advancement it was not the intention of Aurobindo to assert that a race wants nothing. But actually Aurobindo believes in totality of reality. He says, "The world state will give its inhabitants the great advantage of peace, economic well-being, general security, combination for intellectual, cultural, social activity and progress. None of these are themselves sufficient to create the thing needed. Peace and security we all desire at present because we have them not in sufficiency; but we should remember that man has also within him the need of combat, adventure, struggle almost require this for his growth of healthy living, that instinct will be largely suppressed by the universal peace and flat security and it might rise up successfully against suppression. Economic well-being by itself cannot be so heavy as to diminish it appeal and value."[27] It cannot permanently satisfy the human soul.

We can conclude that Aurobindo believes that humanity begins as spirit enters into materiality and able to rise up to spirituality. Similarly the group or social life of individual is the materialisation of the individual but it is also able to rise up and emerges out as free individual. Aurobindo finds the religion, morality to be the material expression of spirit. Even an aesthetic man with flexible thought may not be trustworthy in so far as spirituality is concerned. But individual with test of art and poetry can be the beneficiaries of scientific inventions and modernisation of the world, as it is accepted by him because it adds colour to his life and give a higher social, national or international position to him. Still he fails to reach the stage of cultured humanity as he is dominated by gross vital and commercial desire of a race or a group psychology. But Aurobindo admits that such vital and commercial desires constitute larger part of the social life. Aurobindo also thinks that such life can provide economic well-being, peace and security. But economic and social security is not everything for a human soul which cannot stop from struggling and adventuring. This tendency causes a distraction towards material life of satisfaction and security upsurge towards a higher or different form of life.

Here we can say that the process of spiritual emergence and material expression belong to the same cycle of reality. The cycle moves from materiality to spirituality or collectivity to individuality. Thus commercial, vital, social, religious, moral all worldly affairs of human life belong to the collective or material stage of the cycle. Thus if we try to bring out the relation of man to things or the physical as well as material life it implies not an individual but a collective life. All the effort of keeping individuality while leading a material life seems to be a 'futile effort of man', according to Aurobindo. Such life is capable to bring about a world of humanity. But it is not the final lap of the cycle of the reality.

Section II: Rabindranatha Tagore as compared to Aurobindo is less spiritualistic in his approach. In Aurobindo's discussion the spirituality remain similar to the definition of *Advaita Vedanta, i.e.,* to be known as 'not this not this', spirituality is neither world nor man. In social and economic connotation Aurobindo did not ascribed any affirmative meaning to it. For him it is neither moral nor aesthetic, means it can have no worldly meaning altogether. But when Aurobiundo thinks that to sacrifice one's own individuality is not spiritualism rather materialism then he differs from old school of *Vedanta.* Aurobindo rather considers the free independent individual to be spiritual. But the concept of freedom gets a bit more concrete meaning in Tagore's idea. He says, "Freedom is not darkness nor in vagueness. There is no bondage so fearful as that of obscurity. It is to escape from this obscurity seed struggle to sprout, the buds to blossom. In the same way our soul in order to release from itself from the mist of indistinctness and come out into open, is continually creating for itself fresh fields of action—when men cuts down the pestilential jungle and makes into himself the garden, the beauty that he thus sets free from within its enclosure of ugliness is the beauty of its own soul; *kuvaneveha karmani Jijivishet catam samah*. In the midst of activity alone wilt they desire to live a hundred years"[28] thus through our action only, *i.e.,* by making our inner self out we enjoy freedom according to Rabindranath. He also says, "We stand before this great world. The truth of our life depends upon our attitude of mind towards it. It guards our attempt to establish relations with the universe either by conquest or by union, either through cultivation of power or through that of sympathy."[29] But Rabindranath was not consistent in believing the world as a guiding principle in establishing relation with itself as he thinks that we can transcend this relation. Tagore says, "... when we know the multiplicity of things as final truth, we try to augment ourselves with the external possession of them; but when we know the infinite soul as the final truth, then through our union with it we realise the joy of our soul."[30]

Tagore finds people either to be closely related to the nature despite the dangers, devastation, and barrier in it which is the common feature of the tribal people or to dominate it which is the features of the science. Tagore says, "When we know the world alien to us—then we set up our machines and our methods to deal with it and make as much as profit as our knowledge of its mechanism allows us to do. This view of things does not play us false, for the machine has its place in this world. This aspect of truth cannot be ignored; it has to be known and mastered. Europe has done so and reaped a rich harvest. According to Indian view the highest purpose of this world is not merely living in it but knowing it and making use of it. But realising our own selves in it through expansion of sympathy; not alienating ourselves from it and dominating it, but comprehending it and uniting it with ourselves in perfect union."[31] Rabindranath finds this unity to be completed in the work of art. In such relation artist is not lost in world nor alienated from the world. Only the beauty of the world is capture in the canvas or sculpture.

Once, Rabindranath was shocked at the sight of the river *Ganga*, in Calcutta, at both sides of which there were factories of gunny bags. He admits their indispensability but he believes in the limited use of it and in the importance of leisure for man and a space for joy and worship. Otherwise we will lose our love for beauty, truth and justice and our fellowmen. Rabindranath did not find in the origin and development of Calcutta to be majestic, noble or romantic. He says, "The only thing which gave her the sacred baptism of beauty was the river. Otherwise Calcutta has turned into an office and centre of commercial transactions. Tagore says, "In recent centuries a devastating change has come over our mentality with regard to the acquisition of money. Whereas in former ages men treated it with condescension, even with disrespect, now they bend their knees to it—with the help of science—the whole of human world—has felt the gravitational pull of a giant planet of greed with concentric rings of innumerable satellites causing in our society a marked deviation from the moral orbit."[32]

Rabindranath did not ignore the proper sphere of science which analyses the construction of the world, but world as a creation is not a mere construction for Rabindranath. Even in such a science dominated situation men themselves are used as a material and the human relationship are measured in utilitarian scale. Tagore says, "The prevalence of the theory which realises the power of the machine in the universe, and organises men into machines like the eruption of Etna, tremendous in its force, in its out burst of fire and fume; but its creeping lava covers up human shelter made by the ages and its ashes smother life"[33] Thus we can see that the ever rising materialistic attitude makes man homeless, acquired power of man gives him scientific and commercial success but deprive him of peace.

We can discuss the wonderful description of 'home' by Tagore here. Home is a permanent representation of loyalty and love, free from competition and jealousy. Thus he says, "The permanent significance of home is not in the narrowness of its enclosure but in an eternal moral idea. It represents the truth of human relationship. It reveals loyalty and love..."[34] Rabindranath pointed out that discovery of settlement come with the discovery of agriculture. Nomadic pre-agriculture life is a life for-exploration and exploitation of the world and its contents whereas cultivation of land is exploration of time and leisure. Rabindranath compared agricultural life with nomadic life and find agriculture life to be more secured and certain in terms of both morality and resources. He says, "...agricultural civilisation—is essentially a civilisation of human relationship of the adjustment and mutual obligation."[35]

This is to be noted that though initially man changed his occupation from hunting to agriculture but in today's civilisation we hardly find the instinct of sympathy etc. of agricultural life but an instinct of nomadic exploitation. Today's civilisation by killing leisure and pursuing opportunity is marching ahead with unhampered freedom for acquiring wealth. Tagore says, "Its burden is the burden of things, which grows more heavier and complex everyday, disregarding the human and the spiritual."[36] Tagore pointed out that such civilisation influencing all spheres of life, affecting relationship in and outside home. Tagore says, "Habituated to deal with the world as a machine, man is multiplying his materials, banishing away his happiness, sacrificing love to comfort which is an illusion."[37]

Above culture is originated from western civilisation according to Rabindranath. Question arises how this nomadic life developed into such culture dominated by love for things and machines and addiction to comfort by crating a cleavage more and more wide everyday, in human relation. His realisation of the life of travelers can express how nomadic life develops into a culture dominated by the greed for land and things and not by love for human relationship. Tagore says, "It is not always profound interest in man that caries travelers nowadays to distant lands—the modern age has brought the geography of the earth near to us, but made it difficult for us to come into touch with man—when we fall into the habit of neglecting to use the understanding that comes of sympathy in our travels—easily become unjust and cruel in character. Dealing between different races of men generated according to special historical circumstances—the caste idea is merely institutional—it adjusts human beings according to some mechanical arrangements—it emphasizes the negative side of the individual."[38]

Rabindranath finds western ancient civilisation to be differential, narrow and mechanical. Similarly Rabindranath considered city life responsible for such divisive culture. He says, "The civilisation of ancient Greece was nurtured in city walls. The walls leave their mark deep in the mind of men. They set up a principle of 'divide and rule' in our mental outlook which begets in us a habit of securing all our conquest by fortifying them and separating them from one another. We divide nation and nation, knowledge and knowledge man and nature."[39]

In India the thing was different. The civilisation in India starts by worshiping nature out fear and gratitude for its being hazardous and rich in resources respectively. Aryan invaders took shelter in forest and by them and by the old habitants the Indian civilisation was originated. Tagore says, "...by having constant conjunction with nature the aim of Indian sages was to realise the great harmony between the spirit of the man and the sprit of the world. Subduing nature and achieving things by wrestling with it may be the pride of Westerners. Such habits and training creates an artificial dissociation between him and the universal nature within whose bosom he lies. It is like bud and the blossom into two separate categories and putting their grace to two different and artificial principles, but an Indian mind has never mind never has any hesitation in acknowledging its kinship with nature—was not simply a philosophical speculation—it was her life object to realise this great harmony in feeling and action."[40]

Tagore does not think that thing cannot be valued individually. He does not even think that man is not be rated higher than things of the physical world.

But he does not believe in a universe which is simply humane. He says when man leaves his resting place in universal nature, when he walks on single rope of humanity, it means either a dance or a fall for him, he has ceaselessly to strain every nerve and muscle to keep his balance at each step...."[41] But Tagore believes that superiority of man does not consist in his power of possession of things but in the power of union, it means he has to come out of his narrow necessity and realize its place in the infinite.

But modern civilisation is oblivious of the infinity of the nature. The more civilised a nation is the more energy it spends to get hold over the nature or other races. Thus Tagore says, "Man can destroy and plunder, earn and accumulate, invent and discover but it is dire destruction of him when he envelops his soul in a dead shell of callous habits and when a blind fury of works whirls round him like eddying dust storm, shutting out the *horizon*."[42]

Rabindranath holds that the soul or Brahman, the Upanisadic concept is not a mere abstraction or negation of all in the world but a realisation of the presence of spirit in everything. He quotes, "I bow to God over and over again who is in fire and in water, who permeates the whole world, who is in annual crops as well as in the perennial trees."[43] Tagore thinks that man does not acquire rights through larger space but his right extends through his consciousness of the world through poetry, philosophy, science, art and religion. In order to be conscious of the reality man has to free himself from the bounds of personal desire, and prepare oneself for his or her social duties. Tagore finds an ethical basis of Upanisadic teaching which has to be translated in action. He quotes, "The

Supreme Being is all pervading therefore he is innate good in all."[44] This idea of reaching all pervading truth or spirit through action is not a mere play of imagination for Rabindranath, but "[45]liberation of consciousness from all the mystification and exaggeration of the self."

For Rabindranath action is not a bondage to them who realised the presence of soul in everything. A thing becomes a source of joy when we can realise its infinity it does not remain as a burden on us. As long as our realisation is incomplete we divide things as good and bad, mine and other's, known and unknown, pleasant and unpleasant. But Rabindranath thinks that all the things are good, pleasant, and joyous. He says, "Truth is everywhere, therefore everything is the object of our knowledge, beauty is omnipresent therefore everything is capable of givine us joy."[46]

Tagore's view of human reality in the world is in a nut shell the love for totality or infinity. Personal bondage or confinement to some profit making business is mechanisation of the human relationship. Winning over other races by higher scientific achievement all are the hindrances towards realisation of the infiniteness of the nature. Rabindranath does not deny the superiority of man over other animals and things of the world. But man will destroy his superiority if he tries to capture or dominate nature. He will fail to prove his power of realisation of the infiniteness of the nature, Rabindranath does not deny that science is a success or achievement of human race. But it cannot divide men from men, race from race. It proves lack of the aesthetic sense of the race in spite of higher scientific achievement. It is the lack of aesthetic sense. *i.e.,* the lack of realisation of the infinity for Rabindranath, makes a division among things as pleasant or unpleasant. good or bad.

Section III: Gandhi unlike Rabindranath holds that world is finite as it is a God's creation. For Gandhi it is real since it is God's creation, it is finite since it is not itself God. Nature is an expression of causal order for Gandhi.

Gandhi believes that is possible for science to find out all the laws governing this universe. He says, "All things in this universe including the sun and the moon and the stars obey certain law. Without the restraining influence of these laws the world would not go on for a single moment."[47] But the source of all law for Gandhi is the God. Gandhi does not consider the world as infinite but believes in a continuity of various forms of life. Thus the world exhibits a continuous process of growth. Gandhi believes that since God is the beginning of the world the end of the world progress is God. Thus he finds the world as a result of a force of the will of God which saves it from destruction and maintains harmony and order in the world.

Gandhi believes that man can do nothing to contribute to nature only he can work by maintaining religious and moral discipline. The nature has provided that *karmasthala* to men where he cannot deny but will to live. Work is of prime importance in Gandhi's thought. Work makes men self-sufficient, diminishes distinction between rich and poor. Work guards men against the exploitation by capitalist manufacturers. We should notice that for Gandhi work is mainly the productive work aimed at producing more food grains or more cloths etc. for one's own use.

We can see how Gandhi's thought is dominated by the principle of work for one's own use. Right from his belief regarding basic education for children to running of the national or international government or in his philosophy of *ahimsa* or truth Gandhi is said to be influenced by the doctrine of *karma* of *Gita*. *Gita* preaches in favour of *niskama karma* where work should be done with the spirit of worship of god. Similar view is upheld in Gandhi's philosophy regarding every aspect of life.

Gandhi believes that education cannot be an activity of intellect only. He believes that education has to grow with the surroundings and human body. He says, "Our education has to be revolutionalised. The brain should be educated through the hands. If I were a poet I could write poetry on the possibilities of five fingers—those who don't train their hands, who go through the ordinary rut of education, lack of music in their life. All their faculties are not trained. Even spiritual training is the education of the heart, becomes an abstraction unless there is a happy synchronization between physical and spiritual faculties."[48]

Apart from bodily training Gandhi finds importance of atmosphere of the surrounding in education. He says, "It should be borne in mind that this basic education has grown out of the atmosphere pervades India's seven hundred thousand villages and its millions of inhabitants. Forget them and you forget India."[49] In order to give respect to village as well as to city life Gandhi gave prime importance to the handicrafts. In basic education inclusion of handicrafts will help the city children to understand what a hard work is done by the village people by depending on which city people can enjoy luxury. Gandhi says, "I have not contended that the children of the school of my conception will receive every instruction through handicraft they may be taught—in my scheme of things the hand will handle tools before it draws or traces the writing—literacy is not the end or the beginning of education—literacy in itself is no education. I would therefore begin the child's education by teaching it a useful handicraft and enabling it to produce from the moment it begins its training. Thus every school can be made self supporting—the pupils should therefore learn something about the deep poverty of the masses. They should know the population of India. They should know what is that million should do to their scanty resources. They will understand the virtue of hand spinning—the cause of spinning wheel is too great and too good to have to rest on mere hero worship. It tends itself to scientific economic treatment"[50] Against mass literacy Gandhi expressed his opinion that it cannot increase one's happiness unless education make them self-sufficient. He says, "A peasant earns his bread—has ordinary knowledge of the world—observes the rules of morality—cannot write his own name—by giving him knowledge of letters—will you add an inch to happiness?"[51]

Gandhi contradicts Huxley's concept of education who claimed that a body of an educated youth is servant of will. Gandhi contrarily that conceptual theoretical education could not bring about any change in man's physical tendencies. He says, "The sciences—I have never been use for controlling my senses—it does not make men of us—to do our duty"[52]

Along with this educational idea Gandhi upheld another idea which is known as Bread-labour theory. He holds that one's own bread should be earned by the sweat of the brow. All the people should take part in production. If all the laboured for their bread there would be enough food for all. He says, "Obedience to the law of Bread-labour will bring about a silent revolution in the structure of the society."[53] Through such theories Gandhi tries to involve every body in the production of things of their own use, he equalises, idle sitting and enjoying food and use of other things made by other, with stealing.

But though Gandhi wants all the people to be involved in production but he was against mass production by giant industry or industrialist but was in favour of production by the masses. Industrialism means accumulation of wealth which undermines human values. He was not against machineries but he was against multiplication of machines. Machineries save labour at the same time lead to unemployment. He says, "I want to save time and labour not for a fraction of mankind—

today machinery helps a few to ride on the back, of the millions. The impetus behind it all is not philanthropy to save labour, but greed."[54] He also says, "Machinery is like a snake-hole which may contain one to hundred snakes."[55]

Since industrialisation is a joint phenomenon of civilisation in the world, question arises what Gandhi thinks of civilisation on the whole. Primarily Gandhi is confident that civilisation of India cannot be beaten by the world because it is on the firm basis. In Indian original meaning civilisation means good conduct. Gandhi says, "It is a charge against India that her people are so uncivilised, ignorant and stolid that it is not possible to induce them to adapt any changes. Our ancestors set a limit to our indulgences. They saw happiness was largely a mental condition. A man is not necessarily happy because he is rich or unhappy because he is poor. Observing all these our ancestors dissuaded us from luxuries and pleasures. We have managed with the same kind of plough—cottages that we had in former times. It was not that we did not know how to invent machinery, but our fore fathers knew that if we set our hearts after such things we would become slaves and lose our mental fiber. They reasoned further that large cities will be a snare and useless encumbrance and people would not be happy in them and that there would be gangs of thieves and robbers prostitute and vice flourishes in them...."[56]

What Gandhi expressed as premonition decades ago about large cities, is becoming true today but question arise that how the benefits we are getting by using machines, can be denied? Though Gandhi once said that machines are more beneficial not for the user of it but for the manufacturer of it but we fail to realise it as we are in a dogmatic sleep. Gandhi says, "A man whilst he is dreaming believes in his dream; he undeceived only when he is awakened from his sleep. A man labouring under the bane of civilisation is like a dreaming man. What he actually reads are the works of the defender of modern civilisation which undoubtedly claims among his votaries very brilliant and some very good men. Their writings hypnotise us. So one by one we are drawn into the vortex."[57] Gandhi's main intention was not to denounce machine provided it is not used for cutting down the number of labour employed or used simply for huge amount of production and gather huge amount of money. He says, "How can a country like India with crores of living machines affords to have machines which displaces labours—it would spell the unemployment and ruin—a certain degree of physical harmony and comfort is necessary but above certain level it becomes a hindrance instead of help. The satisfaction of one's physical needs, even the intellectual needs of one's narrow self, must meet at a certain point a deep stop before it denigrates into physical and intellectual voluptuousness. A man must arrange his physical and cultural circumstances so that they do not hinder him in his service to humanity..."

Gandhi opposed capitalism through industrialisation or large scale mechanisation as it makes the division larger between poor and rich and causes exploitation of the poor. At the same time Gandhi opposed bringing about communism or socialism through revolution. He believed in bringing about economic equality through non violence, for this he introduced a new doctrine of trusteeship. That no body can be considered as owner of the wealth but trustee of the wealth will and allow it to be used for the welfare of the society. Economic equality, for Gandhi, can also be achieved by giving the talents its due wages and salary. To bring about equality Gandhi thinks that there should be no class-struggle. Faith, trust, sympathy can do it better. But Gandhi was not very hopeful about the good will of the rich that they will allow the wealth to be spent for the society. Moreover, it is quite a known fact that rich accumulates money through violence or dishonest means. Gandhi says, "Accumulation of money by private person is impossible except through violent means but accumulation by the state in a nonviolent society is not only possible, it is desirable and inevitable."[58]

Gandhi expressed his hope arid faith and the same time his fear for future India. By seeing India's tendency to acquire industrial power and civilisation and on denial of village culture and village cottage industry, Gandhi expressed his agony. He says, "If I can convert the country to my point of view the social order would be based predominantly on the charkha and all that it implies. It will include everything that promotes the well-being of the villagers. It will not exclude the Industries... so long as they do not smother the villages and the village life. I do visualise electricity, ship-building, iron-works, machine making and the like existing side by side with village handicrafts. But the order of dependence will be reversed. Hitherto the industrialisation has been so planned as to destroy the villages and the village crafts."[59]

We can say therefore that Gandhi's philosophy was basically spiritual as he was a God intoxicated man along with strong faith in spiritualism and in the power of the soul. Gandhi in his philosophy of ahimsa upheld this non-violent power of the soul where he denounced the power of the body and violence. But it seems that Gandhi believes in the strength of the body which can work. Gandhi did not denounce the existence of the world like advaitism rather gave much importance to the surrounding world as an object of education and knowledge. Along with though Gandhi does not believe in the revolutionary communism or socialism but he believes in the equality of right on the wealth of the world. He believes that it should be spent for the benefit of the society not for a handful of rich men. For both economic equality and increase in production Gandhi believes in work by all not by machine. If machine has to be used it must be used in the way that it could not increase economic discrimination in the society by making men unemployed but just to decrease the burden of the labour. Thus Gandhi is not in favour of use of the machine for personal interest but for larger interest.

In above discussion no aim is pursued to establish Indian old and modern thought as materialism. Rather it has been tried to point out the concern of the Indian spiritualism about the Physical world.

Along with *Nyaya, Samkhya, Carvaka*, the orthodox philosophical schools and the thinkers inspired by the *Vedanta* philosophy are presented here with their faith in the reality of the world. They find the world as revelation of God. They tried to prove that it is through moral, aesthetic, religious inclination men can do maximum justice not only to the material world but to the whole humanity.

Some Indian philosophical schools consider physical world as identical to spiritual world in actuality and apparently different. Some consider the world to be divine expression, some find it very much independent and original and some find it a source of misery. On the whole excluding one or two philosophical schools we find a tendency among Indian philosophers to make the reader of the philosophy more or less cautious about the outer world nature. World cannot be taken for granted. Only in *Nyaya*, and *Carvaka* philosophy there is no message of caution. *Carvaka* upheld a naturalism which is brute naturalism which has no reason or intellect behind it. *Nyaya* pursued a analytic approach towards nature without relating it to man's spirituality or destiny but by relating it to man's knowing faculty. Buddha and Samkhya find the relation as result of ignorance and *avidya*. Jaina considers knowledge of the world to be infinite as it is relative.

In Aurobindo, Rabindranath, Gandhi we find world to be treated with empathy as it is in itself, so civilisation or industrialisation by spoiling the physical world's original construction is not considered as able to bring about betterment in human life. In their contention due to huge monitory transaction and profit making tendency of the producers, deprivation of section of the society along with natural and indigenous goods, make modern civilisation a half or partial civilisation. It destroys and causes destruction in the divinity of the human world.

In our ordinary way of looking at the world progress we are noticing that it is becoming tougher and more expensive day to day coping with the fast and materialistic development of the society. We can see how sections of the society is getting exploited and marginalised one after another. The situation is caused definitely by the greed to get hold of the things of the world, starting from the luxury goods, money, lands, to the other countries and thereby to get hold even in the air and the sky of the world, *i.e.,* over the whole universe. Everything is grabbed by the moneyed section of the society.

We should not forget that such tendency was not a result of modern industrialisation or civilisation, rather civilisation and industrialisation is the result of such tendencies. This tendency is an age old human tendency, *i.e.,* to acquire money and acquire everything. Question is, by living in such a society of greed and power, how can we save ourselves from being marginalised or finished. The answer we get from the thought of Aurobindo, Rabindranath and Gandhi. If we ponder over it and try to imbibe it in our thought, we can give priority to those things and goods and those machines which are good for greater number and have some humanitarian value in it. We can change our aestheticism by developing a reasonable view about what is good and what is bad. Train, Aircraft, computer network, Television, Print Media—these are expanding human relation provided the governments will use it for the betterment of all the sections of the society. The misuse of it by money making sections may be avoided if people can be philosophically aware.

Despite all these thoughts and philosophies we have been driven by the materialistic wave by centuries after centuries. Human world is a mixture of both right and wrong thinking. If philosophy has to deal with 'what it is then materialistic tendency is the reality. But if philosophy is the realisation of all pervading spirituality then man's materialistic tendency should not cause any harm to the human reality, or this tendency may be considered as an expression of the spirituality only. If Indian philosophy is an age old effort for realising the way to get rid of miseries, then we should find a way within this materialistic world.

In our next chapter thus we will try to analyse and discuss the common men's attitude towards things machines and industrialisation.

References

1. The Life Divine, p. 18.
2. Life Divine, p. 26.
3. *Ibid.*, p. 212.
4. Life Divine, p. 243
5. The Life Divine, p. 108.
6. Life Divine, pp. 759-60.
7. *Ibid.*, p. 446.
8. The Life Divine, p. 506.
9. *Ibid.*, p. 517.
10. *Ibid.*, p. 583.
11. Human Cycle, p. 49.
12. *Ibid.*, p. 49.
13. Human Cycle, p. 49.
14. *Ibid.*, p. 51.
15. Human Cycle, pp. 53-54
16. Human Cycle, p. 74.
17. *Ibid.*, p. 79.
18. Human Cycle, p. 81.
19. Human Cycle, pp. 82-83.
20. Human Cycle, pp. 84-85.
21. Human Cycle, p. 93.
22. Ideal of Human Unity, p. 273.
23. Ideal of Human Unity, p. 273.
24. *Ibid.*, p. 276.
25. Ideal of Human Unity, p. 427.
26. *Ibid.*, p. 470.
27. Ideal of Human Unity, p. 540.
28. Sadhana, pp. 154-56.
29. Creative Unity, p. 45.

30. *Ibid.*, p. 46.
31. Creative Unity, p. 49.
32. Creative Unity, pp. 119-20.
33. Creative Unity, p. 126.
34. *Ibid.*, p. 164.
35. *Ibid.*, p. 165.
36. *Ibid.*, p. 165.
37. *Ibid.*, p. 165.
38. Creative Unity, p. 96.
39. Sadhana, p. 15.
40. Sadhana, pp. 19-20.
41. *Ibid.*, p. 23.
42. Sadhana, p. 29.
43. *Ibid.*, p. 32.
44. *Ibid.*, p. 38.
45. Sadhana, p. 37.
46. *Ibid.*, p. 176.
47. Young India 2.3.1. 1930.
48. Gandhi's Philosophy of Education, R. Shukla, p. 284.
49. *Ibid.*, p. 285.
50. G.P.E. R. Shukla, 293.
51. Hind Swaraj, pp. 87-89.
52. Comparative Ethics of Gandhi and Kant, Dr. P. Kumari, p. 47
53. Hind Swaraj, pp. 88-89.
54. Comparative Ethics of, p. 78.
55. Hind Swaraj, p. 96.
56. Hind Swaraj, pp. 61-62
57. Hind Swaraj, p. 35.
58. G.P.E. R. Shukal, p. 281.
59. Studies in Gandhianism, N.K. Bose, pp. 46-47.

3 Common Men and the Material World

To define the relation between man and the material world of things and activity if it is said that the relation is of interdependence, it will be too simple definition, unable to express the complexity of the relation. More over, in Indian Philosophy this relation is condemned as the source of *dukha*. In this project we have tried to collect some samples of the attitudes of the common men towards the world of things. Along with this we will discuss the attitude of the thinkers like Rabindranath, Aurobindo, Gandhi etc., who did not condemn the attachment to the material world but asked to utilise it by understanding and retaining its spirituality.

We can point out the status of things and the world in spiritual parameter. Tagore considered human body as the temple of the spirituality as the soul resides in it. Aurobindo considered the whole physical world to be the medium of the appearance of spirituality in this world. Gandhi expressed human indebtedness to the nature and blamed human greed for his dissatisfaction. If according to Advaitism or Buddhism the material world and man's attachment to it is responsible for his *dukha* then it seems that these doctrines are suggesting that man should come out of house to avoid being harmed through its destruction. If it is not termed as avoidance but as indifference then question arises what kind of liberation or immortality is it which is indifferent to the world-house and body? No philosophical realisation takes place without this world or human body. So question arises what does transcendental realisation mean? If it is indifference to the material world of things that we could forget things or body or we may use least of it, without being concerned with its illness or well being, deaths and births or natural devastation, it is not at all possible for a human being. If it is claimed that to know thy self or to realise aham brahmasmi is to realise one's identity with the totality then question arises what totality is it. If the totality is that which is not fragmented in past, present, and future or in living and dead then there is no need to make it so abstract with no form no shape no world. If it is said that it is abstract since it is indefinite, not confined to any space or any time, then we can argue that the world of space time is itself indefinite in so far as its origin and expansion are concerned. So knowing thy self not as beyond this world but as within this world, one can realise the identity of himself with the infinity. Profound experience of worldly life can give us the realisation what a huge horizon of unbound reality we are related with. Thus knowing our own self is no less than knowing the whole world or universe. More over every time this horizon is expanding. Thus without being forced to be dissociated from the world we can live a worldly life by knowing the *dukha* as individual as Tagore thinks that mrtyu is individually evil but universally good.

Thus it seems that common men are no less Philosophers in considering the world as a contemporaneous fact with the human being. In this way common men can balance between two extreme thoughts of philosophy Advaitism and Buddhism. Advaitism professes for immortality of the soul by dissociating it from the material world. Buddhism denounced immortality for the impermanence of the world. Common men on the other hand try to achieve immortality and release form *dukha* by knowing the impermanence of this world. Immortality is tried to be achieved by common men by their deeds by next and following generations. This attitude is partly similar to Buddhist view of *Kamma* and partly not because Buddhism does not believe in immortality and rebirth but believe in the continuity of phala in next generation. Actually common men do not believe in rebirth but they believe in continuity of name, fame, and establishment by next generation. Common men may believe in individual impermanence but in eternality of generation and in acquisition of place and position in the world. Question arises why men are not satisfied by the place and position they have already acquired in the world. They go on acquiring more land and multiplying things and money. This tendency of men give rise economic disparity in the society also as all men are not equally capable of acquiring money land fame etc. and clue to the universal crime of depriving and exploiting others.

The realisation of aham brahmasmi can neither be a mere abstraction of all the physical and mental variety of the world nor a mere transcendence from the variety of the world. It can be interpreted as liberation from ignorance. We can say that knowledge of some places or some times is definitely ignorant of the knowledge of ail places and all times. Thus a knowledge which is of place and time in totality is knowledge in the real sense. From empirical point of view we can interpret right knowledge as knowledge of all possible aspects of the human life and the world which is definitely an unending affair of human life. It might be a gradual process or the goal of human knowledge. Since it is a goal cannot be achieved by any empirical means it has to be intuited. But it cannot exclude empirical things and events of the world with which man is engaged for infinite time for generation after generation. So not through sruti from guru or apta purusa but through intuitive understanding of the events of the real world one can realise his soul one with the past, present and future and innumerable births and deaths. Right knowledge cannot consist in transcendence from the life. As Tagore says, "The real training does not consist in foisting moral teaching but in making religion and morality a part of the life."[1]

Aurobinda says, "The teacher is not an instructor or task master he is a helper and guide"[2] In vedantic teaching though the guru must himself be a seer but the empirical embodied life what both the shishya or the guru has to live have not been treated with dignity.

But India from its prehistoric stage bore the rich heritage of using human hand on nature by utilising it in its crude as well as refined forms. Ayurveda by its literal meaning seems to have emerged with the evolution of life. *Caraka* described *ayurveda* as *saswata* and *anadi*. Even the magical power dominated culture of the then period could not rule out the use leaves and roots to recover from the bodily illness.

Indus Valley civilisation also gave evidence of using three forms of drugs from plants animals and minerals. *Sringa vasma* produced out of stag horn was used for cardiac pain and respiratory disorder, samudra phena, the cattle fish bone was used for the disease of ear, *silajatu* produced out of inorganic substance was used to increase body-strength. Bathing in water was given much importance in Indus Valley civilisation.

Ayurveda is taken as *upaveda* of *rkveda* or *atharvaveda*. *Kashyapa* says, "*Ayurveda* is the fifth *veda* and superior to all of them providing number of remedial measures on the practical side." Method of treatment apart from prayer and offerings were discussed in ayurveda coupled with *kaushika sutra*. Application of paste of herbs and oral administration of milk with *laksha* in case of acute injury uses of natural remedy like sunrays fire water etc. proves the use of material and natural world in human life. Arundhati, Arjuna, Aswagandha and many other names we can get which were used as medicinal plants. In Vedic age physiology was studied by elucidating the crucial role of *'Agni'* and *'Srota'*. Entire metabolic process was studied as leading to the formulation of seven dhatus. *Tridosha* of physiological functions pointed out were *bata, pitta* and *kapha.*[3]

In prè-historic age we can get the instances of Indians of using and producing metals. It was named as Calcolithic age using mainly bronze and copper. In the mature stage of Indus valley civilisation in 2750-1900 BC the archaeological evidences show the expertise of metal smith in production in production of copper and bronze. Though extraction of iron was unknown to Harappa but they possess the empirical knowledge of the use of many minerals like lapis, lazuli, turquoise, hematite, amethyst, agate, jasper etc. They did not develop the skill to produce glass but had the skills of glazing pottery. In six to eight century a large pillar *at dhar* of Konarak temple and several iron beams mark the evidence of iron macro technology in India in that time. Barahamihira recorded such metallic composition under the name of *Vajra-sanghata* and described the long lasting durability of the cement applied to temple. Copper and iron apart from being used in jewelry and craft was used in casting of metal religious icons with appropriate iconography and iconolatry.

It seems that men have craved for touching and modifying the material world and its things around him not only for making tools, food and medicines but also for creating a work of art. This tendency of men does not only help him to live better life but also bring him down to miserable life, injury and devastation. We can see that men had to change his tools medicine and food as the days have gone but only his creation of beauty never become old in human appreciation. They remain as a mark of heritage. We will try to throw some philosophical light on this reality later in this project.

In our project we tried to approach the empirical embodied life of the people directly by the method of questioning. We have tried to get the spiritual and intuitive understanding of individual of his empirical life. Urban and rural children and adults are given with a questionnaire to bring out their spiritual and material leaning in their empirical life. Question arises why do we consider questioning as a philosophical method? We should notice that things which are the products of civilisation may not primarily be brought about by industrialisation but through handicraft and small machines made manually. We can thus say that civilisation comes through man's creativity. So if we have to understand civilisation in relation to things we must have a self understanding also. Question is how can we understand civilisation on the whole? It is true

Buddha, Mathura Museum

Avalokiteshwara, Nepal

...gracious imaginations of Bengal, Nepal and Java...

Arjuna Ratha, Mamallapuram

The material in which we work makes its own peculiar demand on the creative spirit, lays down its own natural conditions,...

Bodhisattwa Padmapani, Ajanta

...the unique character of Indian painting, the peculiar appeal of the art of Ajanta springs from the remarkably inward, spiriitual and psychic turn which was given to the artistic conception and method by the pervading genius of Indian culture.

that civilisation is multifarious so we have to identify what civilisation actually is. If we identify it with industrialisation then it would be case of taking a jump defying the stages of the progress of the civilisation. Use of tools in accomplishing day to day work is definitely a mark of civilisation. Water is in abundance in the nature it can satisfy our thirst but the day when we use a glass to drink it up we call ourselves civilised. Thus getting hold and grip over nature seems to be the motive behind civilisation. Daya Krishna[4] defines civilisation as most enduring product of human creativity. Daya Krishna claims that understanding of civilisation is not the understanding of the particular area or field or domain on which man has exercised his creativity over time. It is through self understanding we can understand civilisation. Object of knowledge can be known by knowing the subject of knowledge. No knowledge is unrelated with the action of feeling. All the knowing activities require an emotional commitment. Self knowledge does not only consist in knowing the relation between the self and the world but also in satisfaction and dissatisfaction experienced in this relation and in taken effort in overcoming this dissatisfaction. This dissatisfaction, as claimed by Daya Krishna, provides the dynamic moving force of civilisation unfold in a time, gives specific form or shade thai determines individuality of civilisation. Self reflection is caused by the consciousness that questions, ceaselessly, the unfolding of civilisation, then question every answer to it and give rise to further questions because civilisation is ever alive. No questions have any definite answer, thinks Daya Krishna, so there is the possibility of plurality of answers.

Daya Krishna gives an interesting note on the extent of questioning the intellectual environment of a civilisation. Though there is the possibility of multiple answers but this questioning does not lead to total confusion and disruption of intellectual domain. Daya Krishna finds human being to be conservative and shy of words or ignoring towards answering inconvenient question. Men prefer traditional questions than radical questions. Fundamental questions asked at the beginning of a civilisation have acquired overriding authority and sanctity than questions arising later. The foundational questions thus define and determine a civilisation in deeper sense. Questioning can at least largely influence the freedom of intellectual life of civilisation in later times. Daya Krishna does not try to interpret: civilisation by confining it to realm of intellect alone. He differentiates between self identity and the identity of object. The subjective questioning in relation to the object is totally different from the relation objects have with the world.

Thus we have tried to see whether questioning can be a philosophical method or not, not in the manner in which Socrates or Gandhi dealt with but by giving a questionnaire without intervening or rectifying their thoughts. By knowing individuals attitude towards the world of things we can get some concrete idea about man's relation to, the world of things. Samples may not help us to interpret philosophically the relation between man and things because man may fail to realise his actual attitude and give a wrong answer. People may tend to hide their own view and give idealistic answers then at least we would be able to know what people actually want the relation to be. Now we can go through the different sets of questionnaire.

Questionnaire for children under 10 years, to know how they take the world of things in relation to them

Give answer either by numbering the options as 1, 2, 3...../ write down when it is required.

1. Whose children we are?

   Ans. Our parents/ the nature/ the God.

2. Who gives us life and essentials to life? Our parents/ the nature/ the God?

3. Arrange them according to necessity of our body/ our mind/ our house/ food /clothes/ air/ water.

4. Arrange these man-made things according to necessity; house/ clothes/ food/ water/ soap/ towel/ bag/ shoes/ toys/ television/ computer.

5. Arrange these natural things according to human need; earth or soil/ water/ air/ sunlight/ trees/ fruits/ flowers.

6. Why is the earth so good?

   Ans. It is good because it gives us place to stand on it / grows fruits and vegetables on it.

7. Why water, air and sunlight are good? They are good as they help us to live/ make the world rich and beautiful.

8. Why the trees are good? Trees are good as it makes the nature green/ gives us fruits and flowers.

9. List out the thing in nature or in our house which we can live without; ____________________

____

10. Name some machines which you use; ____________________

____

____

11. The machine you can leave using; ____________________

____

____

12. When do you find yourself related to the whole universe; when you stand under the sky/ sky with stars in it/ you get phone call from your friend from far away?

13. Should we take care of our body/ leave it as it is?

14. Should we make our nature friendly and useful to us/ or leave it as is?

15. What is that thing you like to make in your handicrafts; House/ boat/ kite/ flower/ bag/ garments/ pots/ doll?

Your Signature

Class: ....

Age: ....

First two questions are asked to get the idea how much children are inclined to god or worldly parents. Third to eighth question are asked to know how they rate things, both natural and man made, according to necessity or otherwise and do they have any spiritual or materialistic view about the world. The ninth, tenth and eleventh questions are asked to know how important they consider the things or tools to them. The twelfth question is to know whether through human relation or spiritually they are related to the universe. Thirteenth question is to ask how much important is their body to them, if they can leave it as it is, they will express their spiritual inclination. Next we can go through the questionnaire for children above ten and below eighteen.

Questionnaire for the children from 10-18 years

Tick out/ write down your answer.

1. Do you find the physical world around us like a good neighbour /a rich parent/an unpredictable companion?
2. How do you relate yourself to the nature, by everyday gardening / looking after birds and animals / enjoying the scenic beauty?
3. Do you think that natural disasters are gradually bringing human,world to an end/ human world is an unending reality?
4. What do you think that men are highly developed organism of animals/ representative of god in this world?
5. Do you think that man's body dies but soul does not/ both die together?

The first two questions are asked to know their love for nature and the surrounding world. Third question is to ask the feelings of security in this world. Fourth question is to know their faith in their human self. Fifth and sixth questions are to ask whether they have a spiritualistic or materialistic bent of mind regarding their consciousness of the body. Seventh and eighth question is to know how much spiritualistic and aesthetic awareness they have regarding use of tools and machines. Ninth and tenth question enquires how much they depend on machines and tools. Eleventh and twelfth question is to know their awareness about machines invention and origin and the related human efficiency. Thirteenth question can know how much they rely on their physical and mental ability. Fourteenth question enquires their idea about mechanism, and its utilitarian value.

Questionnaire for adults regarding their attitudes towards the physical world of things

Tick out/ or write down your answer as required:

1. Do you find yourself in the world, as a body in it/ as a mind in it/ as a mind above it/ as a mind-body construction in it / above it?
2. If man has to leave his body and retain his mind, will he die/ be a ghost/ be all powerful?

3. Does man depend 100 % on the natural world/ 80 % on it/ 50 % on it?

4. Give the ratio of the dependence of man on nature and man-made things. 80; 20 or...............

5. How do you rate the man-made things according to necessity; House/ clothes/ food/ stationeries/ accessories/ furniture/ fuels/ electricity/ computer/ television/ refrigerator/ Rails/ aircraft/ personal vehicle/ telephone/ books.

6. What amount of reduction do you think is possible in the use of man-made things by you? ......%.

7. Mark the purpose of using television, computer, aircraf etc. modernity/ speed/ communication/shading of labour.

8. If machines were not expensive it will help all/ ruin all.

9. From the list of things of Q. No. 4 arrange the machines only, according to personal and social utility. ________________

____

____

10. Is production of machine is more beneficial to the user/ the producer.

11. What should be the ratio of saving money and spending money in your choice 50:50 or.............

12. Give a list of the machines you can leave to use :

____

____

13. Is your body a working tool/a hindrance in your path of aspirations?

14. Among vocational activities will you prefer unaided or less instrumental activity like music, poetry, literary work, painting etc./ instrumental activities like weaving, carpentry, machine making etc.

15. Which kind of handicraft or cottage industry do you prefer; spinning or weaving/ poultry farming/dairy farming/ agriculture/ pottery/ carpentry/ book binding.

16. Do you have any definite idea about your requirement of things/ is it increasing gradually as it is produced and marketed by manufacturers?
17. Is there any machine in your imagination, you like to have in this world? Give reasons.

____

____

Your signature.......................................

Occupation..

The first two questions are to know whether men find a soul in themselves if they do, how much powerful they think it to be. Third, fourth, fifth and sixth question is to judge their dependence on the natural as well as man-made things. The seventh eighth and ninth question enquires how much altruistic men are regarding uses of things. Tenth and eleventh question enquires the social as well as economic awareness of common men. Twelfth to fifteenth question enquires how much men are ready to depend on their own body rather than tools or machines. Sixteenth question is to enquire about men's awareness about exploitation by manufacturers. Seventeenth question is to know if common men really have any idea about their requirement of tools or machine or they expect business men to guide them in this regard.

It has been found that children below ten years are sure that they are the children of their parents but get essentials of life from nature. Most of the children rate natural things higher than the man made things as our body need is concerned. Among man made things they rate those things higher, which are used for our livelihood not for entertainment. Earth is important to them as shelter not for its beauty and so on. Sunlight is important for the livelihood to the children. Trees are important for making the nature green not for fruits or flowers. They are in favour of taking care of the body. They are ready and love to live without the machines of entertainment and luxury and a few children dislike unwanted weeds and natural devastation in the world. Astonishingly almost all the children have same view for all the questions except one question regarding their interest in making their own things in handicraft. A few children are interested to make useful things but most of the children are interested to make either flower or doll Those who are interested to make boat or aero plane are found moved and attracted to the vastness of the world but dislike sink weeds or natural devastation. Those who are interested to make flowers etc. are living in a smaller world and attracted to the affectionate human relationship. It seems to me that the children are of two types if we can divide them on the basis of having two philosophical inclinations. One group finds the world vast but accessible and dislikes evils. It seems that they believe in the endless eternal but knowable world. On the other hand another group believes in the love and relationship but neither of the group in considerable number is inclined to believe in god. Regarding their inclination towards the world of machine and tools they are mostly indifferent to it. They don't consider machine to be indispensable. By asking them I came to know that they are interested more in the mechanism and technology of the machine than its utility. It seems that they believe in the precedence of human artifact and planning over machine.

Children above ten years have love for the nature, most of them are ready to perform their duty to the nature by looking after birds and animals they believe in the eternality of the world. They believe in human longevity through his work and mental and spiritual power. Things they find as to bring about well being of man. If betterment does not come it is due to the nature of the things themselves which tends to be out dated. They are ready to leave machines are computer, television and washing machine. They do not think that machine can supersede human talent. In expressing their own choice for making things they consider only making dresses or fashion items and food or artistic object such as model or sculpture. But in reply to the question what machine they can imagine which is yet to be invented, they do not show any practical idea about it.

In case of adults it is found that almost all consider human being to be a mind-body construction but professionals, doctors and engineers does not believe in the eternality of the soul whereas housewives, workers, peasants small businessmen, teachers etc. believe in the eternaiity of the soul. The latter group believes that we depend on nature by cent per cent but the former group believes that we depend on nature by eighty per cent. For man-made things people of both of the groups have expressed variety of ideas in ordering them according to the necessity. People of both the groups consider that reduction in the use of man-made things is possible not more than twenty per cent of the total use. For technologically advanced things like computer, aircraft the professional group holds that it is simply for communication but non professional group finds modernity and speed to be the additional qualities of it. Professionals and small business men think that if machines were inexpensive it would help men whereas most of the non professionals think that it would have ruined all. Both professional and non-professional group find television and telephone for personal use and railway aircraft for social use. Professionals and businessmen think that machine is more beneficial to the user whereas non professionals think that it is more beneficial to the producer. Regarding saving money and spending money most of the professionals think the ratio should be 10:90 whereas most non-professionals think it to be 70:30. Professionals do not believe that they can live without machine but non-professionals think that they can live without television, computer and air conditioner. Most of the persons think that human body is a working tool but housewives, gardener and religious minded people think that body is a hindrance in achieving goal. In choosing between less instrumental and instrumental vocational activity the professional are in favour of latter kind of activity whereas non-professionals are for less instrumental activity. In choosing handicraft most are in favour of weaving. Non-professionals think that they have a definite idea about their requirement of things and machine but professionals think that it increases at par with the production and supply in the market. Neither professionals nor non-professionals have any imaginative and constructive idea about a new machine which can be invented and used by men.

It seems that non-professionals are close to the spirituality and nature and ready to leave at least some of the machines and tools. They have faith in their physical strength. They have the sense of being exploited by the manufacturers and producers. They suffer from the feeling of insecurity and eager to save money. But they do not believe in the possibility of leaving all the machines. They cannot imagine,a new machine. They think they know their limits of requirement of machines and tools. On the other hand professionals admit their dependence on machines. They do not find themselves to be exploited by the manufacturers rather they seem to be indebted to the manufacturers for sophisticated machines and tools. They do not have any idea about inventing new machine except some absurd thinking. They neither have faith in their soul's immortality or physical ability. The businessmen group sways between two such attitudes they believe in immortality of the soul, have faith in god as well as nature and human body, are ready to leave some machines, but they do not find manufacturers to be exploiters. They are in favour of saving more money and spending less. It seems that they aspires to be manufacturers and capture the market but suffers from the feeling of insecurity in investing money for the uncertainty of return...

Above survey shows human dependence on the world of things but at the same time they have a soul which is not in the material world but can transcend itself from the material world and think without machine. Most of them are aware of their being exploited by the manufacturers. Thus machines become a predicament of human life some of which we are born with and some of which we cannot escape but have to live with. But readiness for leaving television etc. seems to express the tendency to be confined into a narrow world. It is a tendency not to expand one's knowledge and contacts this tendency is not against machine but against expansion of human selves. It is a tendency against globalization. But for some of them it is due to the misinterpretation of television or computer as a means of entertainment not as a means of communication, these are treated as dispensable. But we came across people who do not find the requirement of expanding themselves or knowing the outside world apart from that which is needed for their own food, shelter, clothes and entertainment. But we cannot forget that man cannot stop his expansion. Man cannot live simply by his own choice. The return he gets for his choice is other's choice. India could not stop its expansion for several invasion, colonisation and liberation to remove colonisation. We will discuss this in detail in the next chapter.

We can conclude in this chapter that things have a place in human mind as well as Indian thought and culture with rich heritage and also with a mere tendency of running after world development. But Indian thinking faculty does not stop to reflect back and accept a less consuming life. In the following chapter we would try to take a glimpse of the origin and development of consumer life in India.

Some samples of answered paper (women)

Questionnaire for adults regarding their attitudes towards the physical world of things :

Put tick mark or write down youu answer as required:

1. You find yourself in the world as a body in it/as a mind in it/as a mind above it/**as a mind-body** construction in it/above it.

2. If man has to leave his body and retain his mind, he will die/be a ghost/**be all powerful.**

3. Man depends 100% on the **natural world**/depends 80% on it/ 50% on it.
4. Give the ratio of the dependence of man on nature and man-made things. 80; 20 or 95:5.
5. How do you rate the man-made things according to necessity; House/ clothes/ food/ stationeries/ accessories/ furniture/ fuels/ electricity/ computer/ television/ refrigerator/ rails/ aircraft/ personal vehicle/ telephone/ books.
6. what amount of reduction do you think is possible in the use of man-made things 50%.
7. Indicate the purpose of using television, computer, aircraft etc. modernity/ speed/ communication/ shading of labour.
8. If machines were not expensive it will help all/ ruin all.
9. From the list of things of Q. No. 5 arrange the machines only according to personal and social utility. ____________________

    ____

    ____

    ____
10. Production of machine is more beneficial to the user/ **the producer.**
11. What should be the ratio of saving money and spending money in your choice 50:50 or 70:30.
12. The machines you can leave using are____________________

    ____

    ____
13. Your body is a working tool/ a hindrance in your path of aspirations.
14. Among vocational activities you will prefer unaided or less instrumental activity like music, poetry, literary work, painting/ weaving, carpentry, machine making etc.
15. Which kind of handicraft or cottage industry do you prefer;

spinning or weaving/ poultry farming/ dairy farming/ agriculture/ pottery/ carpentry/ book binding, leather work.

16. Do you have any definite idea about your requirement of things/ it is increasing gradually as it is produced and marketed by manufacturers.
17. Is there any machine in your imagination, you like to have in this world? Give reasons.

Ans. ____

____

____

____

A.K. Choudhury

Your Signature

Occuation....................................

Questionnaire for children under 10 years, to know how they take the world of things in relation to them

Give answer either by numbering the options as 1, 2, 3... or write down when it is required.

1. We are primarily the children of; our parents/ the nature/ the god.
2. Who give us life and essentials to life; our parents/ the nature/ the god?
3. Arrange them according to necessity; our body/ our mind/ our house/ food/ clothes/ air/ water.
4. Arrnage them man-made things according to necessity; House/ clothes/ food/ water/ soap/ towel/ bag/ shoes/ toys/ television/ computer.
5. Arrannge these natural things according to human need; Earth or soil/ water/ air/ sunlight/ trees/ fruits/ flowers.
6. Earth is good; as it gives us place to stand on it/ grows fruits and vegetables on it.

7. Water or air or sunlight is good, as it helps us to live/ makes the world rich and beautiful.

8. Trees are good, as it makes the nature green/gives us fruits and flowers.

9. List out the thing in nature or in our house which we can live without; ______________________

____

____

____

____

10. Name some machines which you use;______________________

____

____

11. The machines you can leave using;______________________

____

____

12. You find yourself related to the whole universe; when you stand under the sky/ sky with stars in it/ you get phone call from your friend from abroad.

13. We should take care of our body/ leave it as it is.

14. We should make our nature friendly to us/ or leave it as is.

15. The thing which you like to make in your handicrafts; House/ boat/ kite/ flower/ bag/ garments/ pots/ doll.

Asmita Choudhary and Meghdeep Sen.

Your Signature

Class : VI

Age : 9+

Questionnaire for the children from 10-18 years

Tick out/ write down your answer.

1. Do you find the physical world around us like a good neighbour/ a rich parent/ an unpredictable companion?
2. How do you relate yourself to the nature, by everyday gardening/ looking after birds and animals/ enjoying the scenic beauty?
3. Do you think that natural disasters are gradually bringing human world to an end/ human world is an unending reality?
4. What do you think that men are highly developed organism of animals/ rpresentative of god in this world?
5. Do you think that man's body dies but soul does not/ both die together?
6. Do you think that man lives with the help of his body and things around him/ with his mind, soul and work?
7. Do you think that things are the source of our well-being/ misery?
8. Should we use and enjoy as much things as we can/ as less things as we can?
9. Do you think things can be the source of our misery as there is a chance of losing them/ they themselves can cause misery?
10. Make a list of the things and machines in your house you can leave using Computer, Washing Machine.
11. Is there any machine which can supersede human talent and efficiency? A Machine that can defect future.
12. If you want to make some things by yourself in your handicraft what is it? Jewellery, Woolen Cloths
13. If you have to adapt a handicraft what is it, Spinning and weaving/ carpentry/ pottery/ book binding/ fashion tailoring?
14. Can you imagine a machine which is not yet manufactured?

____

____

Alisha Sen

Your signature

Class : XI

Age : 16+

References

1. Philosophical and social perspective on education by J.C. Agarwal, 2002, p. 56.
2. *Ibid.*, p. 47.
3. Science Philosophy and culture, ed. DP. Chattopadhyaya and Ravinder Kumar, pp. 125-159.
4. Science Philosophy and Culture, ed. DP. Chattopadhyaya and Ravinder Kumar, 1997, Ch. The Plurality of Civilisation and Question of Identity by Daya Krishna, pp. 480-504.

4 The Consumer World

The chapter aims to highlight some historical records of produced and manufactured things in India along with its social, political and economic impact. In this chapter we will discuss the trends of the production of things in India before and after British domination and at the time of it and along with this we will try to analyse philosophically the economic growth of India.

In previous chapter we have discussed Indian heritage *Ayurvedic* medicine and uses of metals as a mark of age old relation of man and thing. We have pointed out that not only for physical need but for aesthetic requirement also things have come into existence. We can see such splendid artistic touch of human hand in Indian monuments, forts, palaces and mansions. These Indian monuments and buildings has led UNESCO to declare some of them as world heritage sites like Taj Mahal, Red fort etc., Apart from that the art and handicraft such as *Pipli, Madhubani, Dokra,* Teracotta have been attracting tourists for centuries. Man and thing relation is not only a mark of civilisation, even *adivasi* community contributed in Indian heritage of art and handicraft. Along *Pipli* etc. we can get some musical instrument like *Dhole, Bansuri* etc. Indian culture has an international reputation for the brass and metal works. The world famous dancing figure of *Nataraj* made of bronze is a piece of art epitomises the achievement of Indian art and culture. Ivory is another material used by Indian craftsmen for making idols, icons, and beautiful lacy designs. India has the deepest ancient mines in the world in the Maski region of Karnataka with carbon dates from 1st millennium BC. Rasaratnakara a text ascribed credit to great Indian scientist Nagarjuna for producing Zinc. Iron seems to have been used in India from about the late second millennium BC. In Khetri region of Rajasthan there is the ancient mines of copper ores from 2nd millennium B.C. Indian cuisine with spices and colourfull ingredient is also a mark of Indian heritage. It has largely been influenced by the invasion of foreigner. Mughal influence is very much on Indian food rich in *ghee*, curd, cream, cashew nuts.

India's rich heritage of architecture, mines, forests rich in honey latex animals and sandal wood attracted inyaders and at the same time it increases the gap between rich and poor. Artisan, mason, carpenter who were the actual contributor to this heritage on meager wages, all coming from village area were being fed on forest and agricultural products. Huge expenses spent on such monuments could have saved and distributed to the poor people. Expensive life style was the cause of the ruination of *Maharajas* and *Sultans* or *Nawabs*. From the very old time India tend to get flourished in cities and towns instead of villages. In old time villages were self reliant but village people were always tend to come to cities and towns for establishment. So in later time some of such expenses have been cut down. It may be due to scarcity of land and over population there has been a, growing tendency for optimum use of land etc. metals are mostly used for machines then utensils then ornaments, not at all for sculpture etc. Only handicraft of indigenous materials and crockery and embroidered garments of Muslim period were remaining popular even now. We can see how the modernising effect of Indian society changed the pattern of production of things in India.

The modernisation of Indian civilisation rests upon three major events in Indian society, first the British colonisation, second the struggle for independence and third the process of transformation going on in India for 62 years after independence to shape its own destiny. Ravinder Kumar discussed the matter under four main headings of cultural, political, moral and economic life. Ravinder Kumar tried to explain the development of Indian civilisation by raising some questions. The first and foremost question he raised was how do civilising and modernising Indians generate the material wealth? Next questions are what are the political and social institutions Indians have devised to conduct and sustain their individual and corporate life? What is the moral vision which shapes their material and spiritual life? Ravinder Kumar admits that such facile simplification cannot help to comprehend the complex totality of civilisation. In first instance he pointed out that in a modernising society mechanism of wealth generation are changing in a concrete manner. In pre-industrial period wealth generation did not have a proper direction. Pre modern societies were largely agricultural but after modernisation much larger proportion of gross product was industrial and utility goods. But one of the striking features of modern society is their orientation to markets. Indian civilisation on the other hand is marked by its extra ordinary longevity for five millennia or more existed through internal evolution and creative interaction with the migrating cultures from outside the territories of India. So according to Ravinder Kumar Indian society was not an inert society which remains unchanged for centuries. But Technological and organisational superiority of Britain over India was the cause of British rule over India. British were not only successful in stimulating production in India but they were also successful in shipping off a substantial proportion of it to Great Britain. Commercialisation of agriculture was started and landed classes were acquiring new wealth but still to acquire the capacity to trigger off economic growth in the country. The artisans continued to produce goods in their cottages rather than in factories. It would be wrong to assume that 18th century was a period of great scientific ferment in India. The problem was that the Indian artisans were not trained to become enlightened and innovative engineers. There was a gap between craftsmen and literate people.[1]

Now we would try to give some lights on the economic scenario of Indian society in British period. The British colonial government did not pursue any active policy of agricultural development except some modest effort to formulate the policy. One such effort was the appointment of Royal commission on Agriculture in 1926. During World War II, disruption of international trade led the government to initiate grow more food campaign. The British government took its 'first agriculture policy statement in the wake of famine in Bengal in 1943. The prolonged neglect of agriculture resulted into no growth in agricultural centre from 1891 10 1946, output of all crops grew at 0.4 per cent a year a rate of food grains was only 0.1 per cent per year. Five year plans after independence increased agricultural production to the 50% of the gross national product. It can be considered as the first phase of the agricultural growth. In second phase India gets independence from foreign food aid. The third phase is identified as the Green Revolution in which India, is made to be a really self reliant country by producing 100 million tonnes of food grains in. 1978 and in consecutive years it increased 10 to 20 per cent up to 1988.

In 1947 the country was poor and shattered. But in 1950 agriculture, forestry and fishing accounted for 58.9 per cent of the GDP and manufacturing was dominated by jute and cotton textile industries. Afterwards public sectors came to dominate heavy industries, transportation and telecommunications. Private sectors used top produce most of the consumer goods but controlled by the government regulations. From 1951 to 1979 Indian economy grew at an average rate of 3.1 per cent a year in constant price. During this period industries grew at an average rate of 4.5 per cent a year and agriculture grew at 3.0 per cent a year. In 1962, 65, 66, 71 India underwent war with china, Pakistan, the world oil crisis, infiltration from East Pakistan respectively. In 1980 to 89 industries grew at 6.6 per cent rate. Agriculture grew at 3.6 per cent rate. From 1947 to 1990 Steel production rose from 1.5 million to 14.7 million tonne a year. Country produced Satellites, Nuclear Power plants. The availability of food again increased 395 gm per day to 466 gm per day. By early 1990s 10 millions of people considered as upper class and 300 millions rose to middle class. In 1980s the growth of the middle class was reflected in the increased consumption of the consumer durables such as televisions, refrigerators, motorcycles and automobiles. In early 1990s domestic and foreign business hoped to take advantage of Indian economic liberalisation to increase the range of consumer products offered to this market. We could take a glance at the growth of Indian manufacturing and thereby the growing demands of the manufactured goods.

Textile industries expanded from 24,000 units in 1951 to 800,000 units in 1989.

Steel produced in public sector is 10 million tonne per year, in private sector 4.7 million tones per year.

Aluminum produced 5,000 tones in 1947 it raised up to 483,000 million tonne in 1992.

Fertiliser industries production reached 7.4 million tonne of nitrogen and 2.6 million tonne of phosphate.

Output of electronic plants and motor vehicles rose from 1.8 billion in 1970 to 123 billion in 1992.

Computer production increased from 7.500 units in 1985 to 200,000 units in 1992.

Energy production is 60 per cent when 90 per cent is required.

Coal production increased from 105 million tonne in 1970 to 320 million tonne in 1992.

Oil and natural gases produced 664.582 barrels per day.

Electric power produced 69, 100 megawatts.

Nuclear power produces 2,320 megawatts of energy.

Railroads extend 62,458 km.

India increased roads from 400,000 km in 1950 to 2 million km in 1992.

In this 960,000 million surface road, 1 million gravel or crust stone road, 20,000 km natural highways.[2]

In the twentieth century the consumer life grew dramatically in consumer life, began in purchasing thing for price. Soon mass production and industrial production came into being. Consumer became market dependent for their everyday needs. It gives the dealer a good reason to exploit them. Products became underweight and inferior in quality and standard.

At the same time a large section of the society looks for food security, assured safe water supply, shelter, education and health service. Only for imported goods and latest models of cars the attraction pertains to very few.

Indian stock for food grains in 2001 were 60 million tonne, yet one third of the Indian population live below poverty line. Consumers often go hungry and remain malnourished. 20-25 per cent of the urban population live in slums or in make shift colonies or in refuge settlement house. In rural area the situation is equally bad. People live in make shift dwellings, without sanitation facilities and running water or electric supply.

Fair price shops in India are 4.5 lacks in number under PDS, on an average of 1:200 ratio. The cause of deteriorating urban life is said to be the environmental pollution. Environment must ensure a lot of open area and parks and gardens, maintenance of wild life and bio-diversity, safe and sufficient water supply, no pesticide-ridden food, no chocking exhausts fumes from vehicles.

But astonishingly the consumption pattern is itself responsible for the scarcity and lack of environment. Monthly purchase of mosquito repellant, toilet cleaning acid, non-biodegradable packets, for pre-packed food products. According to World Bank report India loses 24,500 crores for the cost of environment. People are consuming products like chocolates, syrup etc. without knowing the manufacturing details.

But by the right to information act people can know *(a)* how to consume a product, *(b)* the adverse health effect of its consumption, and *(c)* ingredients are consumer friendly or not.

Products are becoming harmful for the environment when lipsticks etc. are tasted on animals, wages for manufacturing shoes become less, and children are becoming targets for advertiser for promoting sales.

In developed countries the good of the consumer world lies in the variety of choice for the same products because they believe abundance of goods lead to good living. But actually more variety of same product, encourages false variety claim and false sense of choice. Due to increase in competition manufacturers are discovering newer ways of cheating and duping the consumers.

One billion uneducated Indians are the victim of lucrative market of pharmaceutical industry. To boost up sales companies are offering free samples, even free luxury holidays to the physicians to influence, to use, and prescribe their brands.

Consumer should ask himself (1) does he really need this product, (2) how long does he want to use it, will it last that long, (3) what are the health fallout of the product, if it is a food product, does it have five health benefits. Thus consumer can play a important role in checking the market and restricting consumption. Government or manufacturer may not supply all every difficulty all the consumer should buy eco-friendly products and food with high nutrition content.[3]

In India men consumers constitutes the almost total amount of intoxicating food and nonfood product. Some are highly injurious, some are less injurious to their own health hut have high polluting effect in environment and non-consumer health. Rise and growth of a Tobacco company into a corporate sector is a sign of immense consumption of intoxicating item by men.

Indian tobacco Company, ITC was incorporated on August 24, 1910 under the name of Imperial Tobacco Company of India Limited. In 1928 the head quarter Virginia House was situated at Chowrangi Calcutta. From 1974 the cigarette and the tobacco company enters into a wide range of business of hotels, information technology, packaging, paper boards and paper, agricultural-exports, food, life style retailing for men and women comfort wears. In 1990 the company has set up a division of export for agricultural commodities. From 2000 it became a fastest growing global IT and IT enabled services. From 1992 it enters into food business by offering ready to eat food it produces Indian gourmet dishes confectionary, ataa, agarbatti and safety matches. In 2005 it introduced 'Essenxa dewills' and exclusive range of bath and body care products for men and women. 'Fiama dewills' a range of shampoos. In 2007 'Vivel dewills' a range soaps. Thus a cigarette company is producing almost every thing for man and woman's day to day requirement by taking the advantage of the public demand and the tendency to live on manufactured goods.

We can see that from pre and post civilisation era human beings are very much attached to the world of things. Some men claimed a realisation that it is the cause of our dukha but the more men are becoming advanced and developed, are getting more inclined to the uses of things. Today computer and so on has become so much a central point of all human endeavour that computer becomes another soul of human life. If we try to find out the cause behind it we will see either it is human ignorance as it is said by the Indian philosophers or it may be due to the fact of man's being himself a body with mechanism tend to be attracted towards a machine. Our body is a loathsome machine we have to carry it, its being wrong cannot be rectified by us. Our body is partly dependent on us but mostly we depend on our body. Our body has many limitations so we want a helpful machine. Moreover except some natural things all things are man made which astonish us but we like to take part in that genius creation by men. Every scientific discovery finds its success in its being used. It is not only impossible or absurd to think of a human life without the use of a thing but also denying its talents. It is not correct that men are not trying to cut short the uses of things. Men themselves are apprehending possible harm of the consuming world.

But what is the cause of maximum agony is the global warming caused by different scientific experiment and non-biodegradable elements. But it is true that we cannot stop human hand to produce things and use it to get more comfort, more enjoyment, more money, and so on. Man cannot live on basic need. Only earth, water, fire, air cannot satisfy him what tendency is appreciated and praised by Tagore as greater I 'Bada Aami.' Aurobido may not find any difference between greater I and smaller I because for him the higher plane of soul emerges through the lower plane of material world. Gandhi gave maximum importance in bringing up ability to produce things by our own hands. He was against massive industrialisation but never said that things of all sorts are the hindrance towards realisation of the power of human soul. In our next and last chapter we will try to develop a philosophical account of the ideal relation between man and things.

But in spite of massive growth in consumer goods and its consumption a section of the society is still deprived of the thing of basic requirement. They are deprived of the three basic things food, cloth and shelter because ultimately getting and using thing depends on the purchasing power of the people. Indian society is divided into various income groups. All higher, middle and lower groups are divided into sub groups and they have varied purchasing power. Indian society and culture is also a mixture of various customs and rituals and festivals. Thus a wide and exclusive range of production is required to meet the customer's demand. On top of it western influence has increased this buying tendency by adding some more things to the list of consumer market. Right from Indian pujas festivals marriage ceremony all are things oriented. We can see lots of minute things and objects are considered necessary in such occasions. Such customs are responsible for price rise along with the profit making tendency of manufacturers and traders and the weak price control system of the government. This is only responsible for economic inequality in India. If things are necessary then nobody should suffer from lack of things and nobody should have more than his or her requirement. Things should not capture space in our houses as well as in offices or on roads and make our life difficult. We should see how many people can use a same thing for how many times. Our buying should be very intelligent and economical so that we can utilise the maximum benefit of the thing by spending less. We all know that buying long lasting thing by spending a bit more money is always found beneficial to us. Possibility of more choice in the market is not wrong as it resist monopoly. We should shift from one brand to another brand regularly. We need to develop a proper consumer personality which must be aesthetic, conscious, humanistic or at least intelligent alert and self esteemed.

In next and last chapter we will try to develop a rational way of using things. For this purpose, we will try to discuss the philosophical thoughts of Tagore, Gandhi and Aurobindo. We will point out how Tagore relates the outside world to men on an artistic account which he considers to be the real human relation. We will discuss how Aurobindo emphasised on a conscious or supra conscious existence of men which resists him to be relegated to the standard inertia. How Gandhi upheld a theory of bread-labour, *i.e.,* by making one's own thing and thereby resist the both way exploitation of village and worker people by the town dwellers or rich people on the one hand and exploitation of consumers by the manufacturers.

References

1. The modernising Experience of Indian Civilisation: Some Reflections, Science Philosophy and Culture, Ed. by DP Chattopadhyaya and R. Kumar, 1997, pp. 505-516.
2. World Infopaedia, India part II, Pragun Publication, D.K. Publisher Distributers enterprise, 2007, pp. 769-714.
3. Consumer goods. Indiabizclub.com, consumer rights in India, consumer goods and services, law, rights.

5 The World as a Goal

The chapter aims to establish the man and thing relation as a continuous process in which being of the world only is the goal of man. The expression may appear confusing but in Sartre's interpretation, the being of the consciousness is nothingness as it has nothing of itself. He says, "the only monism which starts with the human world and which situates man in the nature is the monism of materiality. It alone is the realism."[1] But question arises do Indian authors agree with it? We have discussed how Indian culture and civilisation grew through the man and thing relation. Natural and man-made things played a crucial role in the physical, psychological, aesthetic, religious and social development of an Indian. We can say this relation has three levels. Primarily it lies in the usage of things and in the exploitation of the nature; secondarily, in attachment to the things and love for nature and natural beauty and finally in creativity through artistic and technological pursuit of human beings. This man and thing relation is marked by abundance and scarcity. Some things are in the hands of some people in abundance and on the other hand some are deprived of some thing. Both of the situations are unacceptable. Thus man and thing relation is a relation implies a struggle, an effort to acquire more, and this effort causes a serious problem in human reality. This is not the case that only deprived are struggling but privileged are struggling as well. One become exploiter of the others and makes them revolutionaries. The whole human society suffers tension, anxiety, bloodshed and so on. If the requirement or proper distribution of material things is concerned then question arises who will make the distribution proper? This question remained unanswered as communism which literally means equal consumption has failed to succeed in world political scenario. Power actually means the power over the property of the world so how an empowered let other to have as equal as he.

J. Krishnamurty sounds extremist when he says that we look at the tree with a utilitarian purpose, there is no love for earth only usage of earth. But he is right when he says that to be is to be related—the world and I are not separate entity—the world is my own extension—to understand the world is to understand myself. JK thinks that understanding is not possible by condemnation or justification but by going into the relationship. JK rightly pointed out that scarcity frustration etc. come through political exploitation religious rituals and profession and business. Men are always exploited by politicians, priests and experts. We should avoid being guided by leader's thought, stop repeating religious practice. About profession and business he brings modern technological advancement into discussion. He points out that the means of production is in the hands of a few. In political world there are conflicting nationalities, fear and threats of war. There is technological advancement without vital psychological advancement. The modern world is of cultivated intellect and empty hearts. Human faculty is marked by technical physical and administrative tricks and not by creativity. The transformation of the outside world is not the task of specialist, leaders or priests rather we have to bring about radical transformation by our creativity. In order to be creative we must know the world and our relation to the world. We cannot withdraw ourselves from the world. We have to understand ourselves and the significance and the meaning of our relation with thing, people and ideas. But there is no end of self knowledge. Self knowledge is moment to moment.[2]

In Sartre's interpretation this perpetual understanding of self is due to perpetual appearance of the world as consciousness is perpetually directed to it. He says, "The thought of a human being situated in the world and acted upon by all the cosmic forces, one which speaks of the material universe as something which is revealed gradually through *praxis* in *situation*."[3] In the Critique Sartre is interested primarily in the social conflicts arising among groups in the milieu of scarcity. Question is why there is scarcity. Sartre does not consider the world itself to be responsible for this but the human 'praxis' in this world. He says, "The world has not created me;—me has not created the world. These are two objects of absolute impersonal consciousness, and it is by virtue of this consciousness they are connected."[4] He also says, "It would be necessary to think of the world, conceived as the synthetic totality of all things. Sometimes we do indeed apprehend the world beyond our immediate surroundings as a vast concrete existence. The things that surround us appear only as the extreme point of this world which surpasses them..."[5] Sartre holds that consciousness exists as a process of intending objects and the ideal unity of consciousness is the material world itself but it is ordered by consciousness which exists as world only when revealed to consciousness. So Sartre says, "...In the universe every existence is material, in the world of man everything is human."[6]

We can see both Sartre and J. Krishnamurty are of the opinion that scarcity is caused not by the material world but by the human activity. We can remember Gandhi's famous saying in this context that nature has produced enough for human need but not for human greed. Thus we are bestowed with the task of knowing ourselves along with this world. Our personality in terms of our socio-psychological make up is the reason behind the world being poor or rich. We can discuss Aurobindo, Rabindranath and Gandhi in this regard who claim the realisation of the universal truth about man and world relation.

Aurobindo thinks that life is neither an inexplicable dream nor an impossible evil, because it is the principle of matter on which the life stands upon. Even the mental and supra-mental existence of man are conditioned by the body and matter because man has developed or given a body and a brain capable of receiving and serving progressive illumination and risen above animals, above himself and reach the divine manhood. Aurobindo also says, "Life has not really defeated by the matter—mind is not victorious over life and matter, but has only achieved some imperfect development of some of its potentialities at the cost of others. Aurobindo believes that earth's existence cannot be the result of human-mind rather human mind itself is the result of earth existence but he believes that both human mind and the earth are created by universal mind. But at the same time Aurobindo says that sharp division between matter and spirit has no fundamental reality. Spirit is the soul and the reality of that which we sense as a matter. Matter is the form and body which we realise as spirit. The ascent of man is physical to supra-mental which opens to the corresponding ascent in the grades of substance from matter to the ideal or causal body of our supra-mental being.[7]

On the basis of above philosophical realisation Aurobindo suggests a powerful new creation in all fields as our great need. He thinks that India can only survive by casting modern aggressive world into the mould of her own spiritual ideals. Social and political liberty, equality democracy etc. are to be accepted not because they are modern and European but because they are the things of greatest importance in the future development of man's life. It must be assimilated into our culture but not crudely but by going back to whatever correspond to it and justify it in our own spiritual conception of life and existence. Aurobindo says, "Mentally, vitally and physically I do not grow by a pure self development from within in a virgin isolation;" he upholds that in every individualised existence there are self development from within and reception of impacts from outside. The second process is not harmful for the first if the inner genius is not too weak to deal victoriously with its environmental world.[8] A true happiness is the right terrestrial aim of man lies in the maintenance of natural harmony of spirit mind and body. Civilisation with this harmony lies in the material intellectual and spiritual progress, in Europe material comfort, progress and efficiency becomes the Gods of worship. Aurobindo thinks India should stop penetration of such culture. Regarding the question of unified world-culture, Aurobindo suggests that India should preserve the spirituality through gradual development. In this gradual development the first stage is of conflict and competition between past and present overshadowed by the past. The second stage brings the concert or unity with a free differentiation not by swallowing up of one by the other. The third stage is for Aurobindo is of sacrifice it belongs to the indeterminate future in which self-defense and attacks are needless, here all beings are known as one.[9]

Aurobindo finds the above characteristics in Indian art which will reveal the Indian perspective in relation to the object and creativity. Excellence of Indian art is beyond dispute not in a sense of individualised beauty but in a sense of generalised beauty. Indian art expresses spiritualism and make all other thing a subservient to and means of spiritual growth of the people. Aurobindo says, "Taj is not merely a sensuous reminiscence of an imperial amount or a fairly enhancement hewn from moon's lucent quarries, but a dream of love that survives death. The figure of Buddha achieves the expression of the infinite in a finite image, the illuminable calm of *nirvana* in a human form and visage. *Nataraja* is the majestic expression of dance at calm and stillness. Paintings of Ajanta express simplicity in the greatness of power.[10]

Thus we could say that it is inevitable for men to be related to the world of things Indian as well as European thinkers are pointing out how man and thing relation is shaped and designed by human point of view. The essence of this relation does not consist in the individual point of view taken on it but in the universal and impersonal view point. If we would like to walk on the path of progress we should follow the method of assimilating past into present, material into spiritual and thereby West into East.

Nataraja, Tanjore

The Buddhistic, the Vedantic seeing of things may be equally powerful starting-points for artistic creation, may lead one to the calm of a Buddha or the other to the rapture dance or majestic stillness of shiva...

Sundaramurti Swami, Colombo Museum

The dignity and beauty of the human figure in the best Indian statues cannot be excelled, but what was sought and what was achieved was not an outward naturalistic, but a spiritual and a psychic beauty...

Taj Mahal, Agra

The Taj is not merely a sensuous reminiscence of an imperial amour or a fairy enchantment hewn from the moon's lucent quarries, but the eternal dream of a love that survives death.

Kandarya Mahadeo Temple, Khajuraho

The great temples of the north have often... a singular grace in their power, a luminous lightness relieving their mass and strength, a rich delicacy of beauty in their ornate fullness.

Cave Cathedral, Ajanta

The secular buildings of ancient India, her palaces and places of assembly and civic edifices have not outlived the ravage of time; what remains to us is mostly something of the great mountain and cave temples, something too of the temple of her ancient cities off the plains...

Humayun's Tomb, New Delhi

It seems to me that here the Indian mind has taken in much from the Arab and Persian imagination and in certain mosques and tombs. I seem to find an impress of the robust and bold Afghan and Mogul temperament; but it remains clear enough that it is still on the whole a typically Indian creation with the peculiar Indian gift.

Itimad-ud-Daulah's Tomb, Agra

Not rational but magical beauty satisfying and enchanting to some deeper quite suprarational aesthetic soul in us is the inexpressible charm of these creations.

Dhyani Buddha, Ajanta

The figure of the Buddha achieves the expression of the infinite in a finite image,... the illimitable calm of *Nirvana* in a human form and visage.

Maheshwara Murti, Elephanta Caves

The inspiration, the way of seeing is frankly not naturalistic, not, that is to say, the vivid, convincing and accurate, the graceful, beautiful or strong, or even the idealised or imaginative imitation of surface or terrestrial nature.

Nagaraja and Queen, Ajanta

The sculptor must express always in static form; the idea of the spirit is cut out for him in mass and line, significant in the stability of its insistence...

Kalahastishwara Temple, Andhra Pradesh

The straight way here is not to detach the temple from its surroundings, but to see it in unity with the sky and low-lying landscape or with the sky and hills around and feel the thing common to both, the construction and its environment, the reality in Nature, the reality expressed in the work of art.

Rabindranath Tagore gives a detailed account on this relationship. Tagore holds that we are face to face with this world and this great world is manifold. One of this is the necessity we have to live, to till the soil, to gather food, to cloth ourselves, to gather materials from nature. We are always making things that will satisfy our needs. Then we have our mind and mind seeks its own food, here mind is bewildered by the heterogeneity of things and cannot find a unifying principle. Mind does not find only facts but some laws to lighten the burden of mere number and quantity. There is yet another man in every body who is not physical but personal. The personal man is found in the region where we are free from all necessity. It has personal relations of its own with the great world and conies to it to satisfy its personality. This is the world of reality what we feel with our emotion. This is the world, for Tagore, from which science turns away and art takes place. Art, like life, grows by its own impulse. Fixing the value in art by something is not inherent in it. The excellence of the river cannot be judged by the value of a canal. Tagore finds it futile to define art but worthwhile to question the reason of its existence and enquires whether its origin owes to some social purpose or need to cater our aesthetic enjoyment. An animal for Tagore is limited to its need but Tagore says, "Man—in life commerce is a big merchant. He earns a great deal more than he is absolutely compelled to spend. Therefore there is a vast excess of wealth in man's life which gives him the freedom to be useless and irresponsible to a great measure. This surplus seeks outlet in the creation of Art, for man's civilisation is built upon his surplus. The man with strong religious feeling not only worships his deity with all care but his religious personality craves, for its expression, the splendour of the temple., the rich ceremonials of worship.

When we are in poverty, Tagore points out, all our attention fixed outside us for the object we need. But when our wealth surpasses our need, we feel we are rich. This efflux of consciousness of his personality requires an outlet of expression. Therefore in Art man reveals himself not his objects. Thus the contents of the personality of man consist in how it is related to the outer world. This apparent world is man's world. It has taken its special feature of shape, colour and movement from the peculiar range and qualities of our perception. Not the physical or chemical forces but man's perceptual forces are its potent factors, because it is man's world arid not the abstract world of physics or metaphysics. It becomes completely our own when it comes into our range of emotion. With our love and hatred, pleasure and pain, fear and wonder continually working upon it, this world becomes a part of our personality. It grows with our growth, it changes with our changes. We are great or small according to the magnitude of our assimilation. If the world is taken away, our personality will lose its all content. Tagore quoted Upanisad, "Wealth is dear to us not because we desire the fact of the wealth itself, but because we desire ourselves". This means that we feel ourselves in our wealth,—and therefore we love it.[11]

Tagore also pointed out another side of human beings by showing that man cannot help revealing his personality, also in the world of use. Here self expression is not our primary object. When in everyday life we are moved by habits we are economical, in our expression—glide on its accustomed grooves. But when our heart is fully awakened in love or emotion then our personality is in its flood-tide. Man's energies, running on two parallel lines—that of utility and of self-expression—tend to meet and mingle. By constant human association sentiments gather around our things of use and invite the help of Art to reveal themselves,—as we see the worrier's pride and reveal in the ornamental sword-blade and the comradeship of festive gatherings in the wine goblet.[12]

We can point out some difference of Tagore's thought from Aurobindo, Krishnamurty and also Sartre. Except Tagore neither of them encourages luxury in terms of self expression and spirituality. It seems that Tagore does not believe in any restriction on human freedom even if man expresses some sort of irresponsibility towards everyday life of utility and so on. When Taj is an expression of faith in immortality for Aurobindo, for Tagore it seems to be an expression of emotion with splendour and wealth, it seems that both are true in their own contention, it seems that the faith in immortality is expressed through splendour and wealth otherwise there would have been no Taj. But such a marvelous work of art, such an attachment to things as a medium of expression of love, faith and emotion cannot be defined simply as materiality which attracts and astonished people from all over the world for centuries. Something is there in every work of art even in handicraft which makes them immortal what we do not find in the objects of utility. Objects of utility and even the factories produce such objects are getting obsolete by the passage of time.

Here we can discuss **Gandhi** who found things and the making of it as essential means of training mind. Gandhi's philosophy was not romantic like Tagore, not claiming reality in any sort of conscious drive like Sartre and not even highly sophisticated in spiritual expression like Aurobindo, rather Krishnamurty is close to Gandhi. Gandhi's Philosophy can be defined as applied spiritualism what we find in his concept of Ahimsa. He discards weapons to win over enemies, discards highly sophisticated machines or tools, even disregards industrial civilisation but did not discard things of day to day use. Peculiarly claims that making such things and tools by themselves student can develop a better human being in themselves. He thinks that real education has to draw out the best from the boys and girls. This can never be done by packing ill assorted and unwanted education in the heads of the students. It becomes a dead weight crushing all originality in them and turning them into mere automata. He claimed for himself, "I would develop in the child his hands, his brains, his soul—I hold that true education of the intellect can only come through a proper exercise and training of the bodily organs, *e.g.,* hands, feet, eyes, ears, nose. I want the whole education to be imparted through some handicraft or industry. My idea is not to teach a particular profession but to develop the full man or woman in a student. The brain must be educated through hand. It is not by making our brains a store-house of cramming facts that our understanding is opened. An intelligent industrial training is often a more valuable aid to the intellect than an indifferent reading of literature. Self sufficiency is not a prior condition. This does not mean the basic education will be self supporting from the very start. But it is the acid test removing the discrimination between working class and educated and at the same time income and expenditure must balance each other. Students must not be caged. This does not mean they are not subject to discipline. But discipline has nothing to do with artificial restraint upon students' all round growth. Gandhi opposes the idea of corporeal punishment on students as he considers the body as a temple of god.[13] But Gandhi finds him only educated, whose intellect is clear, cold, logic engine with all its parts of equal strength—whose mind is stored with knowledge of fundamental truth of nature. Who has learnt to hate all vileness and respect others as he respect himself. Such a one and no other, I conceive has had a liberal education, for he is in harmony with nature.[14]

Tagore has some similar view on education he holds that a school should be situated in natural surrounding. Education should cultivate love for nature among the students. Students should be educated on sewing, book-binding, weaving, carpentry etc. Educational institutions should have dairy firm, post office, bank, hospitals and workshop in its own campus and students are allowed to utilise this offices and institutions. Though students must get an atmosphere of *Tapovan* means surrounded by forest in their educational institute but they need to avail and learn to utilise the governing system of the country.

We have seen that all the thinkers have given much importance to the earth and man relation. They have given importance to the things of the out side world not because they are serving our purpose but because they are the expression of the universality. By knowing them we will know our actual selves. They have given importance to both body and mind and training of the body and mind and that can be done only by relating ourselves to the out side world of things, people and ideas. This relation is aimed at the betterment of the human life as well as betterment of the world around us. The aim should be to put an end to the exploitation of the nature and the unprivileged section of the human society.

References

1. Critique of Dialectical Reason, Tr. By Alan Sheridan-Smith, London, NLB, 1976, p. 248.
2. On Nature and The Environment, J. Krishnamurty, Penguin Books, 1992, pp. 1-10.
3. Critique, p. 126.
4. Transcendence of the Ego, Tr. By P. William & R. Kirkpatriek, NY, Noon Day Press, 1957, pp. 105-06
5. Transcendence of the Ego, pp. 74-75.
6. Critique, p. 248.
7. Life Divine, Sri Aurobindo, pp. 276-312.
8. The Renaissance in India, Sri Aurobindo, pp. 43-45.
9. *Ibid.*, pp. 57-60
10. The Renaissance of India, pp. 255-314.
11. Personality, Lectures delivered in America, Macmillan, 1917, reprinted 2001, pp. 11-23.
12. Personality, p. 25.
13. Philosophical and social perspective on Education, J.C. Agarwal, Shipra, 2002, pp. 88-91.
14. Hind Swaraj or Indian Home Rule by M.K. Gandhi, Navajivan Publisher House, Ahmedabad, 1938, p. 88.

Conclusion

We can conclude that human relation to this world of things is gradually endangering the relation itself. It is not all that we have to take care of the outer world or animals rather we have to understand that we are the children of this world. We have created things as we are the part and parcel of creation. Things cannot be described simply as products by the destruction of nature and indulgence in luxury. There is an internal attachment between man and things. All the imbalances among different groups of men in the use of things are caused by money and political power. If the moneyed class can go to buy things directly to the artisans the gap decreases. But too much of production of wooden materials silk or wool is endangering the lives of related species. Artisans, weavers and business men are found to collect huge amount for sell and without being able to sell off all the things go for discount sale. These are all the tendencies to become rich by single chance. On the other hand customers are loading their houses with that much of things of which they need only a meager amount. Breaks in familial relations, has also increased the need of things for individual family or person.

We have seen that Indian Philosophy is not materialistic but by accepting primary eternal elements of nature, causality and evolution it has shown the concern for nature and its eternality. Accepting the nature does not mean accepting materialism. But Philosophy cannot avoid materialism a predominating phenomenon of the human reality. Indian Philosophy cannot avoid the rich heritage of medicine, sculpture and architecture. But still man is not oblivious of the truth that less consuming life is the better life for human being as well as nature.

It seems that it may not be possible in any near future for men to stop using nature for its luxury and well being. But men should know what his actual well being is. The well being must continue as long as human reality will continue to exist. Well being cannot confine to a specific time and place. Well being is a universal well being. We need to imbibe thoughts of humanitarian thinkers like Aurobindo, Tagore and Gandhi in our thought. Aurobindo finds inanimate like 'Taj' or statue of Buddha as the expressions or love for infinity or immortality. Tagore thinks that man can be fully expressed only through his work of art. He also says that every object of our love is nothing but love for ourselves. Our personality cannot be devoid of the outside world. Gandhi professes in favour of becoming one with all of our physical organs and the world for our proper development. He does not believe in any human development which is simply intellectual. We should give matter a spiritual value for its manifesting power which has made human race a worldly phenomenon. We should appreciate and preserve its beauty and grandeur unconditionally. We should involve all of us in the making of things because the world is not something alien to us, rather it is our parent and our own house.

Bibliography

1. A History of Indian Philosophy, S.N. Dasgupta, Vol. I and III, Cambridge, 1951, 52.
2. Capital Structure and Corporate Control, Ranjul Rastogi, Anmol Publication, 2001.
3. Changing Perspective on Creativity, Professor Sajida Zaidi.
4. Computer Education, U.K. Singh, K.N. Sudarshan Discovery Publishing House, 2005.
5. Comparative Ethics of Gandhi, and Kant, P. Kumari, Classic Publishing Company, New Delhi, 1996.
6. Contemporary Indian Philosophy, B.K. Lal, M.B. Publisher Pvt. Ltd., Delhi, 2002.
7. Corporate Philosophy in India, P.N. Srivastava, Pointer Publication India, 1989.
8. Creative Unity, R. Tagore, Macmillan Pocket, Tagore-Edition, 1988.
9. Crisis in Civilisation, Tagore, Visva Bharati, 1941.
10. Education for All, Achieving the Goal Vol. I-III, The Global Consensus, APH Publishing House Corporation, 2007, D.B. Rao.
11. Effective Teaching Method, A Hand Book, S.R. Vashist, Mangal Deep Publication, 2003.
12. Encyclopedia of Education of 21st Century, Ed. B.M. Sharma and A.S. Sharma, Commonwealth, 2008.
13. Future of Man, Spirituality, Science, Culture and Civilisation, M.L. Dhawan, Classic Publishing Company, 1996.
14. Gandhian Philosophy of Education, R. Shukla, Sublime Publication, Jaipur, India, 2002.

15. Hindswaraj, M.K. Gandhi, Navajivan, Sarvodaya, 1958.
16. Hinduism and The Clash of Civilisation, David Frawley (Vamadeva Shastri), Voice of India, New Delhi, 2002.
17. Indian Philosophy by S. Radhakrishnan, Vol. II, Oxford University Press, 1989, 7th impression 2008.
18. Indian Philosophy S. Radhakrishnan, Vol. I and II, Macmillan & Com., London, 1951.
19. Indian Philosophy, A Survey (1917 - 1942), J. N. Sinha, Progress of Indian Studies, Ed. R.N. Dnadekar.
20. Introduction to Indian Philosophy, S.C. Chatterjee Cal., 1948.
21. Krishnamurty the Years of Fulfilment, Mary Lutyens, A discus book, Published by Avon Books, 1948.
22. Krishnamurty Reader, Ed. by Mary Lutyens, Penguin Books, 2002.
23. Lokayata : A Study in Ancient Indian Materialism, D.P. Chattopadhyaya, Cal., 1948.
24. Materialism in Indian Thought, K.K. Mittals Munshiram. Memorial Publisher Pvt. Ltd., New Delhi, 1974.
25. On Nature and Environment, J. Krishnamurty, Penguin Books, 2005.
26. Outlines of Indian Philosophy, M. Hiriyana, London, 1951.
27. Personal Excellence through the Bhagvat Geeta, S. Sukhobodhananda, Jico Publishing House, 2008.
28. Philosophical and Sociological Perspective on Education, J.C. Agarwal, Shipra, 2002.
29. Philosophy and Curriculum, M. Edger, D.B. Rao, Discovery Publishing House, 2003.
30. Philosophical Enterprise and the Scientific spirit, G.C. Nayak, Ajanta Publication.
31. Philosophical Essays, P.R. Damle, Asia Publication House, Bombay, 1954.

32. Philosophy of Common Man, T.N. Dhar, Rajat Publication, New Delhi, 2003.

33. Philosophy, Physics and Cosmic Play, Ramanarayna Vyas, Ajanta, 1992.

34. Problems of Philosophy, ed. by S.P. Dubey, ICPR, New Delhi, 1996.

35. Sadhana, R. Tagore, Macmillan Pocket, Tagore Edition, 2000.

36. Sarvodaya, Navajivan, 1958.

37. Science and the Modern World, A.N. Whitehead, Cambridge University Press, 1953.

38. Studies in Jainism, Dr. Jacobin, Ed. by J. Muni, Ahmedabad 1946.

39. Six Systems of Indian Philosophy, Maxmuller, London, 1916.

40. The Art of Living, M.K. Gandhi, B.V.B., Bombay, 1961.

41. The Central Conception of Buddhism and the Meaning of the Word Dharma, London, 1923.

42. The Changing Times, A Commentary on Current Affairs, M, Godbole, Orient Longman, 2000.

43. The Guru of Joy, Sri Sri Ravi Shankar and The Art of Living, Francois Gautier, Hay House India, 2008.

44. The Human Cycle, The Ideal of Human Unity, War and Self Determinism, Sri Aurobindo, Pondichery, 1962.

45. The Philosophy of Jean Paul Sartre, Ed. by P.A. Schilpp, Southern Illinois University, Carbondale, 1997.

46. The Religion of Man, Tagore, Introduction by Andrew Robinson, University Paperback, London, 1988.

47. The Renaissance in India, Sri Aurobindo, Pondichery, 1997.

48. The Vedanta, N. Dutta, Calautta, 1931.

49. Towards Universal Man, Tagore, Asia Publishing House, Bombay, 1961.

50. Vedic Science and Culture in India, H.C. Sharma, Book Enclave, 1999.

51. Vocational and Technical Education, D. Thakur and D.N. Thakur, Deep and Deep Publication Pvt. Ltd., 2004.

52. Vocational Guidance of Elementary School, S.R. Vashist, Anmol Publication Pvt. Ltd., New Delhi, 1995.

53. World Infopaedia, India, Part-1, 2, 3, Penguin Publication, 2007.

Index